Counseling
and Psychotherapy
of Religious Clients

Counseling and Psychotherapy of Religious Clients

A Developmental Approach

Vicky Genia

PRAEGER

Westport, Connecticut
London

BF
51
. G45
1995

Library of Congress Cataloging-in-Publication Data

Genia, Vicky.
    Counseling and psychotherapy of religious clients : a
developmental approach / Vicky Genia.
        p.   cm.
    Includes bibliographical references and index.
    ISBN 0–275–95107–3 (alk. paper)
    1. Psychology and religion.   2. Psychology, Religious.
3. Pastoral counseling.   I. Title.
BF51.G45   1995
158′.3′0882—dc20   94–37888

British Library Cataloguing in Publication Data is available.

Library of Congress Catalog Card Number: 94–37888
ISBN: 0–275–95107–3

First published in 1995

Praeger Publishers, 88 Post Road West, Westport, CT 06881
An imprint of Greenwood Publishing Group, Inc.

Printed in the United States of America

The paper used in this book complies with the
Permanent Paper Standard issued by the National
Information Standards Organization (Z39.48–1984).

10 9 8 7 6 5 4 3 2 1

Contents

Preface

I always considered myself to be a religious person. I attended church faithfully and frequently participated in prayer meetings and Bible study groups. Until I experienced an emotional crisis, I never questioned my religious convictions. However, a series of setbacks shattered the hollow security of my simple-minded devotion.

Upon disclosing my doubts and concerns to a trusted minister I was told that my suffering and disillusionment resulted from my lack of faith. The reality of the traumatic losses and disappointments in my life were glossed over with formulas for instant peace. I was urged to "cast my cares upon the Lord" as if God can be used as a garbage disposal for unwanted problems and frustrations.

When my supplications failed to provide emotional relief, feelings of guilt for my faithlessness caused me to become even more despondent and confused. I was convinced that God had either abandoned me or was punishing me for my failures and doubts. Finally, I sought professional psychological help. It took me several years to work through the psychological conflicts that were underlying my depression. In the process my faith was transformed.

I learned from my experience in therapy that my problems of faith had more to do with damaging childhood experiences than the unfortunate circumstances that precipitated my spiritual crisis. My professional training and clinical work have corroborated my earlier discovery that an individual's religious experience is considerably intertwined with his or her psychological make-up. Faith draws on the psychic resources that are constituted in the earliest experiences of life. When we are adequately nurtured as children we are more likely to develop a healthy spiritual outlook.

I believe that regardless of our particular religious allegiances, our faith evolves through five distinct stages over the course of a lifetime. However, some people fail to progress beyond the earliest stages and cling to outmoded or distorted beliefs. This book describes the psychological characteristics that are typical of people in each of these stages and emphasizes that childhood experiences play a critical role in our spiritual evolution.

I approach the subject of faith from a psychological rather than a theological perspective. While not denying the importance of religious and cultural influences, a life-affirming faith is highly contingent upon a healthy psychological outlook. Spiritually healthy and unhealthy people are found in all faith traditions.

A goal of this book is to help professional caregivers respond more effectively to clients and counselees who exhibit unhealthy or destructive forms of faith. Traditional mental health practitioners in particular are loath to attend to religious matters in therapy. It is hoped that the theoretical model and practical suggestions presented in this text will help psychologists, social workers, marriage and family therapists and professional counselors feel more confident about entering the client's religious domain when appropriate.

This work is also relevant to pastoral counselors, members of the clergy and other religious professionals. I have seen dedicated and compassionate ministers, priests and rabbis become bewildered and frustrated over certain congregation members who continually falter in their faith despite competent religious guidance and assiduous efforts to promote spiritual healing. By understanding how faith can be poisoned by negative childhood experiences, religious professionals will be better equipped to respond to their counselees' and parishioners' problems and needs.

I claim no special authority on spiritual matters. My humble wish is to share with other professional helpers the ideas and insights that have evolved from my work with those whose faith was transformed through emotional healing. An understanding of how spiritual concerns may be linked to underlying psychological conflicts can be helpful to anyone who counsels spiritually committed people.

Counseling
and Psychotherapy
of Religious Clients

Chapter 1

Introduction

The academic study of religion is rarely an aspect of the therapist's training and the overall attitudinal matrix of a psychology-oriented education tends to foster a negative attitude toward religions.

Robert Lovinger
Working With Religious Issues in Therapy

With few exceptions, traditional psychotherapists have been subservient to Freud's assessment of the religious life as neurotic and self-deceptive. As a result, they often fail to meet the needs of religious clients. With a recent resurgence of interest in religion and spirituality, secular psychotherapists are challenged to become more attuned and responsive to their clients' spiritual values.

Whereas traditional therapists tend to regard all religious thinking as illusive, religious professionals often fail to appreciate the psychological significance of disordered religiousness. It is time for traditional and pastoral caregivers of all religious faiths to relinquish their adversarial positions and become more versatile in their therapeutic efforts. This book is an effort to raise the consciousness of all professionals who counsel spiritually committed individuals.

A major premise of this book is that formative relationships with early caretakers exert a tremendous impact on the spiritual life of the individual. Depending on the quality of these formative experiences, adults may develop highly evolved spiritual beliefs, or they may fail to progress beyond the magical and illusory faith of early childhood. Case studies are presented that illustrate how damaging religious beliefs are linked to early psychological trauma. The particular therapeutic issues that clients are likely to present at various phases in their spiritual development are also elaborated.

Although a psychodynamic orientation undergirds this approach, my work is also informed by the strong humanistic and existential thrust of my graduate training. Psychoanalytic readers will notice that my clinical style deviates from strict therapeutic neutrality. I believe that the "real" bonding that unfolds in the human-to-human encounter is a more potent curative factor in therapy than transference analysis. In some cases a nurturing relationship with an empathic and a genuine therapist serves as the impetus for positive transformations in the client's bond with the sacred.

Because the spiritual enterprise is a highly complex, subjective and deeply personal phenomenon, it does not lend itself easily to scientific investigation. Contemporary quantitative research methods fail to capture the breadth and depth of the individual's experience of the sacred. Therefore, I rely heavily on case studies and clinical observation. Despite the limitations of the case study approach, many theoreticians, including Sigmund Freud and William James, have contended that the psychology of religious experience is best illuminated through in-depth analysis of the personal histories of spiritually observant individuals.

I should emphasize that the general thrust of my work reflects Western spiritual thinking. The psychospiritual development of individuals who are raised in Eastern religious traditions may be very different from those exposed to Western faiths.

Finally, to avoid conceptual confusion it is necessary to clarify some key terms. For purposes of this book "secular psychotherapy" refers to therapeutic approaches derived from the theoretical formulations of traditional, mainstream psychology. "Secular psychotherapists" are trained in traditional psychology-oriented programs and use psychodynamic, client-centered and behavioral interventions in treating emotional distress. The theory and practice of traditional secular psychotherapy when not openly antagonistic toward religious values have, for the most part, excluded the spiritual dimension. Although the humanistic and existential paradigms are informed by therapeutic assumptions that are congruent with ethical and spiritual values, humanistic psychotherapists may not be sympathetic toward traditional religious faiths.

In contrast to secular psychotherapy, "religious counseling" is predicated upon the ideals of a particular religious tradition. Religious counselors help their clients attain healthy emotional and religious functioning as defined by a shared theological framework. Whereas secular therapists normally do not disclose their personal spiritual beliefs to their clients, religious counselors and therapists actively promote a particular religious world view.

The terms "religious" and "spiritual" are used interchangeably in recognition that many who are oriented toward the transcendent or sacred may not affiliate with organized religion. Since this discussion focuses on the personal drama between the individual and his or her conception of the transcendent, this distinction is not critical.

This book is not an exhaustive text on the psychology of religion. It provides a tentative model for understanding the links between an individual's spiritual life and his or her developmental history and offers guidelines for the psychological treatment of individuals at various phases of their psychospiritual development.

The value of this work will be judged not only on its theoretical and practical significance, but also on whether or not it contributes to greater integration between psychology and religion and, most important, whether or not it stimulates further collaboration between traditional mental health practitioners and religious professionals. Dr. James Jones, who is both a philosopher of religion and a clinical psychologist, suggests that dialogue between psychology and religion is most fruitful when it

grows out of the lived experience of those who have religion and psychology as part of their lives, from practitioners, not from uninvolved theoreticians, from those who struggle to live out a spiritual path and are immersed in the actual practice of psychological research and treatment, those whose theorizing is informed by their practicing.[1]

This book is largely a result of my own efforts to straddle the boundary between psychology and religion. If this material stimulates further reflection and exploration of this topic, my efforts will be well rewarded.

NOTE

1.   James Jones, "Living on the Boundary Between Psychology and Religion," *Psychology of Religion Newsletter, American Psychological Association Division 36* 18 (1993): 6.

Chapter 2

The Nature of Faith

There is hardly a word . . . which is subject to more misunderstandings, distortions and questionable definitions than the word "faith."

Paul Tillich
The Dynamics of Faith

Any attempt to incorporate faith into psychological theory must begin with some preliminary assumptions about the nature of faith. A comprehensive analysis of this topic is beyond the scope of this book. However, a brief discussion will serve to orient the reader to the material that follows in later chapters.

Faith refers to the individual's way of responding to a transcendent power. A person's sense of the sacred may or may not be associated with a particular religious allegiance. While religion helps many people to nourish and express their faith, religious belief or practice is not synonymous with faith itself. Many religiously unaffiliated individuals feel anchored to an ultimate reality and attuned to a higher purpose.

As with other abstract concepts such as love, freedom and equality, it is easier to articulate what faith is not than to present a concise definition of what faith is. Although it is not my intent to reduce such a complex phenomenon to a collection of negatives, by qualifying what faith is not we are better equipped to assess the spiritual health of our clients.

First, and perhaps most important, faith is not certainty. People of all religious traditions encounter storms of doubt. By helping the pious to purge themselves of outmoded and destructive religious ideas and beliefs, skepticism serves to enhance and revitalize their faith.

Second, faith is not allegiance to a given set of propositions. During my spiritual crisis I was admonished for my failure to "believe in the Lord." My emotional distress was glossed over with platitudes about "accepting the Word" and "having faith." However, one does not *have* faith. One *lives* faith.

Gordon Allport, a prominent figure in the psychology of religion, distinguished between intrinsic and extrinsic religious motivations.[1] People who are extrinsically motivated use religion for self-serving means. They may flaunt their piety in order to receive approbation or feel morally superior. In contrast, people with an intrinsic spiritual orientation attempt to live their faith. Research studies consistently show intrinsics to be psychologically and emotionally healthier than extrinsics, regardless of religious affiliation. These studies suggest that *how* an individual believes is more important for emotional well-being than *what* he or she believes.

It is also important to emphasize that faith is not feeling. Faith in a transcendent reality may at times produce intense emotional and perhaps even mystical experiences. William James, in his classic work *The Varieties of Religious Experience*, written at the turn of the century, stated that "emotion convicts before logic convinces," implying that feeling is the cornerstone of spirituality.[2] Indeed, people who are intrinsically committed to their spiritual ideals experience feelings of reverence and devotion. However, faith is not synonymous with religious sentiment. The spiritually mature remain steadfast in their convictions despite fluctuations in mood.

Human emotions are elusive and unpredictable. Particularly intense feelings such as those experienced during moments of heightened spiritual awareness, romantic excitement or aesthetic pleasure do not sustain their intensity for more than relatively brief periods of time. Mystical experiences are reported to last no more than a few hours at most. Biographies of spiritual leaders depict the fluctuating nature of their moods. It is not uncommon to discover that the emotions of the most pious oscillate between ecstatic sensations of mystical unity and overwhelming feelings of abandonment and despair. Therefore, feelings of reverence alone will not support a sustaining sense of spiritual solidarity.

Contrary to popular belief, faith is not blind. It is not a magical leap out of darkness into sudden illumination. The spiritually mature make an informed commitment to a self-chosen faith that is congruent with their inner convictions.

To some extent we choose a particular religious allegiance because it intuitively appeals to us. James Fowler, who has written extensively on faith development, refers to this quality of faith-knowing as the "logic of conviction," as distinguished from the "logic of rational certainty" by which an object or event is known through cognitive reasoning alone.[3] The Biblical definition of faith as "the substance of things hoped for, the evidence of things not seen" (Hebrews 11:1) also alludes to the transrational quality of spiritual conviction. However, to admit that faith supersedes human logic does not imply that all religious thinking is illusive or blind.

To clarify this point let us examine how trust is inspired in human relationships. When we meet someone we like, we advance to deeper levels of intimacy slowly and cautiously. In the beginning our interactions are superficial. We discuss the weather or news events, and we share nonthreatening information about ourselves. If the other person responds with warmth and acceptance, we disclose more personal information as the relationship deepens. We may eventually establish a close, intimate relationship as we learn to trust one another.

Just as trust in interpersonal relationships is not based on "blind love," but develops as people share personal information about themselves, trust in a higher reality grows in direct proportion to the amount of knowledge we possess, however incomplete. Therefore, the intellectual quest for truth is an important aspect of mature faith.

Finally, faith is not resignation. Many religious groups encourage their members to submit to a higher authority. In Christian theology the believer who surrenders the "old self" is promised regeneration into a "new self" through God's grace. Other religious traditions encourage their adherents to forfeit worldly desires in order to purify their souls and unite with the Divine.

In order to grow psychologically, emotionally and spiritually we must relinquish less mature or unhealthy ways of thinking and behaving. Personal regeneration thus requires a renunciation of the immature parts of the self so that a more mature and adaptive new self may emerge and develop. Because it is human nature to cling to the safety and security of familiar ways of thinking and behaving even when they are maladaptive and self-destructive, this transition into greater maturity is never easy. Many people overcome destructive habits and behavior patterns by refocusing their energy toward spiritual ideals.

The religious literature is replete with accounts of dramatic personal transformations through spiritual "conversions." Many recovered alcoholics will attest to the healing effects of trusting in a transcendental force. However, the Alcoholics Anonymous twelve-step program does not encourage participants to become passively dependent on their higher power. Alcoholics who are committed to their recovery implement each of the twelve steps in a disciplined and systematic manner. In other words, alcoholics submit to a higher power in order to gain greater control of their lives. The idea that surrender and willful effort are not mutually exclusive is emphasized by William James in a footnote to his treatise on conversion.

Starbuck is right when he says that 'self-surrender' and 'new determination,' though seeming at first to be such different experiences, are "really the same thing. Self-surrender sees the change in terms of the old self; determination sees it in terms of the new."[4]

In other words, reliance on a divine Other is not an inactive submission of will, but an active redirection of will. The spiritually observant individual does not relinquish self-responsibility, but willfully "attempts to harmonize his life with the Beyond."[5]

A comprehensive definition of faith was not attempted here. My intent was to present ideas about faith that are relevant to people of divergent spiritual beliefs. Although sketchy and incomplete, these basic assumptions provide a starting point for theory building.

NOTES

1. Gordon Allport, "Behavioral Science, Religion, and Mental Health," *Journal of Religion and Health* 2 (1963): 187-197; Gordon Allport and J. Michael Ross, "Personal Religious Orientation and Prejudice," *Journal of Personality and Social Psychology* 5 (1967): 432-443.

2. William James, *The Varieties of Religious Experience* (New York: Penguin Books, 1985).

3. James Fowler, *Stages of Faith: The Psychology of Human Development and the Quest for Meaning* (San Francisco: Harper & Row, 1981), 102-104.

4. James, *Varieties*, 214-215. Quoting Edwin Starbuck, *The Psychology of Religion* (New York: Scribner, 1899), 160.

5. Walter Houston Clark, *The Psychology of Religion* (New York: Macmillan, 1958), 254.

Chapter 3

Psychological Perspectives on Faith

Traditional psychological theories of human behavior indiscriminately pathologize individuals with strong religious convictions. Psychoanalytically oriented therapists in particular tend to be persuaded that all religious or spiritual conviction is illusive and neurotic. Strongly influenced by Freud's thinking about religion, many psychoanalysts believe that reliance on God is an outmoded continuation of childhood dependency.

Infants and young children perceive their parents as omnipotent, god-like figures. Children are especially prone to idealize their fathers on whom they rely for protection and support. Although healthy adults relinquish their childhood illusions, Freud contended that most continue to long for someone to protect and comfort them. He concluded that this universal need for a surrogate father is the psychological force that draws people toward religion.

Thus, from a psychoanalytic perspective, religious practice is a neurotic repetition of early childhood. Since the world is frightening and unpredictable from the moment of birth, Freud theorized that the human race created an exalted Father in order to feel protected and secure. According to Freud, the pinnacle of human enlightenment will be achieved when this universal illusion is vanquished by science.

Despite the fact that much of Freudian theory is anathema to behavioral psychologists, many share Freud's negative evaluation of the religious life. Aversion toward religion and spirituality has been particularly rampant among cognitive-behavioral psychologists, a sub-group of the behaviorist school, who emphasize the importance of cognition in determining human behavior. In contrast to psychoanalytically oriented therapists, who link psychological dysfunction with childhood trauma, cognitive-behaviorists relate emotional problems to distorted thinking patterns.

Cognitive-behavioral psychology proposes that negative emotions and interpersonal problems stem from irrational beliefs that we have about ourselves or our world. For example, the belief that we must never displease others will cause us to be unassertive and overaccommodating in our interpersonal interactions. Some of these irrational beliefs were taught to us by our parents or other significant people in our lives. Other beliefs were assimilated through social and cultural norms and the influence of the mass media.

Following the antireligious bias of Albert Ellis, founder of rational emotive therapy, many cognitively oriented psychotherapists presume that all religious beliefs are irrational and immature. For Ellis and his followers, atheism is the only road to optimal emotional health and well-being.[1]

Finally, humanistic-existential psychology represents a "third force." Even though the humanistic and existential paradigms diverge on several fronts, theorists of both persuasions admonish their behavioral and psychoanalytic colleagues for being deterministic and reductionistic. In contrast to those trained in the more traditional models, humanistic and existential psychotherapists see much of human behavior as self-determined and consciously directed. Individuals are thought to be propelled by an inner thrust toward growth and maturity.

On the surface a humanistic or existential psychological orientation seems more compatible with religious or spiritual values than either the psychoanalytic or the behavioral perspective. Since the humanistic-existential paradigm is a more loosely organized system of psychological thought, it lacks a coherent theory of spiritual belief. However, the issues that are central to existentially focused therapy such as mortality, freedom and responsibility, isolation and intimacy and ontological meaninglessness parallel the concerns of all major religions.

Nevertheless, humanists tend to regard the transcendent as nothing more than a higher level of consciousness. Research indicates that many humanistic psychologists are religiously unaffiliated and do not believe in a supernatural power. Consequently, humanistic and existential practitioners may be as unsympathetic toward traditionally religious clients as psychoanalytic or behaviorally oriented therapists.

This brief summary fails to do justice to the breadth and complexity of our psychological traditions. Moreover, few practitioners rely exclusively on one particular theoretical orientation. Most clinicians are skilled in a variety of methods and vary their approach in accordance with the client's needs. It is assumed that most readers are familiar with these theories. They are presented in abbreviated form in order to encourage readers to become more attuned to their feelings and attitudes about religion.

Traditional psychological services are underutilized by the deeply religious who fear that their beliefs and values will be undermined or ridiculed. The tendency to pathologize faith stems from the fact that clinicians have ample opportunity to observe the high correlation between psychopathology and deranged religiosity. From these observations theorists erroneously assume that religion is the cause of mental illness. Contemporary psychologists of religion, however, believe that it is the nature of the psychic organization that determines the spiritual health of the individual. Disturbed religious functioning is the external manifestation of pathological tendencies in individual believers.

Some types of religious expression are undeniably unhealthy, and their pathological nature is obvious even to the casual observer. Examples are the person suffering from a delusional disorder who claims to be the Messiah and the person who believes that a voice from God commands him to commit criminal acts. Less extreme examples of disordered religiousness are depicted in emotionally constricted, dogmatic individuals who berate themselves for their imperfections and normal human emotions.

Without denying that some religious groups do seem to promote healthier attitudes than others, it cannot be presumed that religion itself is responsible for an individual's hallucinations or delusions. Spiritual conviction does not cause religious delusions any more than political allegiance causes ordinary people to perceive themselves as famous political figures. Rather, emotionally unstable people unconsciously express their disturbance in religious or political language. Depending on the delusional individual's developmental history, he or she may assume the identity of a religious savior or a renowned political leader. In either case psychotic thinking results from mental illness, not from religious or political affiliation.

Admittedly, some religious communities are healthier than others. In some cases emotional disturbance can be exacerbated by harsh or deranged religious indoctrination. Nevertheless, emotionally unstable people are often drawn to destructive religious communities where they can reenact their emotional traumas.

Psychology's tendentious view of religious faith is rooted in Freud's indictment of religion as "the universal obsessional neurosis of humanity."[2] It is important, however, to keep in mind that Freud formulated his theories from observations and analyses of emotionally disturbed people. Therefore, his ideas about religion were profoundly influenced by his immersion in unhealthy forms of religiousness. Freud's conclusion that all religious faith is neurotic resulted from his failure to recognize religiousness as a developmental process and to discriminate mature from less evolved forms of spiritual expression.

Notwithstanding that conversations on religion within traditional psychological circles tend to be disparaging, a vocal minority have vigorously challenged religious stereotypes. Inspired by such notable figures as William James, Carl Jung, Gordon Allport and Erich Fromm, psychologists of religion have labored to provide a more sophisticated understanding of how religion interfaces with personality development and mental health.

Perhaps the most important insight gleaned from this work is that faith is not a simple, one-dimensional trait, but a highly complex, multifaceted phenomenon. Although some spiritually committed people do use religion in unhealthy ways, others develop a faith that vitalizes and sustains them. Allport's distinction between intrinsic and extrinsic spiritual motivations has already been mentioned. Others who distinguished mature from immature modes of spiritual expression include Fromm, a Neo-Freudian psychoanalyst who contrasted a defensive, authoritarian religious outlook with a healthier, more flexible humanitarian spiritual orientation,[3] and James, who discriminated "healthy minded" believers from "sick souls."[4]

These early efforts to differentiate psychologically healthy spiritual orientations from neurotic and self-deceptive forms of religiousness challenged the presumption that religious conviction is necessarily an inauspicious sign. However, in order to work effectively with religious clients, some important questions need to be addressed.

Why are some people authoritarian in spiritual outlook and others humanitarian? Why are some spiritually committed individuals intrinsically motivated and others extrinsically oriented? A starting point for answering these questions involves assimilating ideas from developmental psychology into our psychological theories of religion.

NOTES

1. Albert Ellis, "Psychotherapy and Atheistic Values: A Response to A.E. Bergin's 'Psychotherapy and Religious Values,' " *Journal of Consulting and Clinical Psychology* 48 (1980): 635-639.

2. Sigmund Freud, *The Future of an Illusion* (New York: Doubleday, 1927), 77-78.

3. Erich Fromm, *Psychoanalysis and Religion* (New Haven, Conn.: Yale University Press, 1950).

4. William James, *The Varieties of Religious Experience* (New York: Penguin Books, 1985).

Chapter 4

Psychospiritual Development

If young children are exposed to religious teachings, their faith is dominated by the normal narcissism that characterizes the age of innocence. They beseech God for special favors and distinguish right from wrong by expectations of reward or punishment. Magical thinking, fantasy and comfort-seeking pervade the religious expressions of young believers.

God images of children are fashioned from their relationships with parents and significant others. Therefore, abused children are likely to view God as formidable and ruthless. Conversely, children who are adequately nurtured and affirmed will perceive God as loving and compassionate. In the minds of young believers God is an extension of the parental dyad.

Without the ability to think abstractly or employ logical reasoning, young children assume that religious stories, parables and myths are literally true. If they attend worship services, the peculiar sights and sounds may either frighten them or arouse their curiosity. Until they are able to symbolize their experiences, young believers imitate religious rituals and recite formal prayers with little comprehension of the spiritual implications of these practices. Since they are still under the illusion that they are the center of the universe, very young children may feel psychically merged with this strange Other who has so completely captured their parents' attention.

To observe that children are egocentric is not to imply that they are intentionally selfish or insensitive. On the contrary, healthy young children show a great deal of affection and concern for others. By egocentric we mean that perceptions of others are under the dominion of the child's needs and wishes.

Although normal for young children, egocentric faith in adulthood is a developmental aberration. If it were true that all religious individuals were spiritually egocentric, then Freud's assessment of religion as illusive and immature would be correct. However, Freud's analysis can be challenged on two fronts. First, this distortion of faith is not universal. Many religiously committed adults present more evolved forms of faith.

Second, Freud's psychological analysis of egocentric faith in adulthood is erroneous. Freud believed that faith in God was rooted in a universal inability to relinquish the protection and nurturing we receive from our parents. Thus, adults confronting their powerlessness in a threatening world, and longing to recapture the feeling of security they experienced as children, create a divine caretaker.

The error in Freud's thinking lies in his assumption that adequate parental nurturing perpetuates the child's longing for protection long after he or she is grown. Contemporary psychological theory holds that just the opposite is true. It is those children who are deprived of sufficient nurturing who continue to seek it in adulthood. If the child's early milieu was not safe, he or she will grow up feeling insecure and defenseless and may turn to religion for comfort and protection.

Conversely, children reared in families that are reasonably stable and soothing develop a basic feeling of confidence in themselves and others. Adults who experience a sense of connection with an affirming world do not feel compelled to seek surrogate caretakers. Having outgrown childhood needs, the spiritual lives of healthy adults are transformed into more mature forms.

The guiding supposition of this book is that the vicissitudes of psychological development have a profound impact on the individual's spiritual life. Before proceeding to propose a developmental typology of faith I must emphasize that human development is a lifelong process that is never completed. The endpoint of maturation is a conceptual ideal that even the most spiritually endowed can only approximate. Furthermore, development does not always progress linearly and smoothly. When we experience a crisis or prolonged frustration of our needs, we may regress to earlier, less mature ways of coping. Additionally, some people mature in spurts with long plateau periods intervening between peaks of rapid growth.

Notwithstanding idiosyncratic variations and individual differences, psychospiritual development generally appears to progress through five distinct stages. Under ideal conditions a person's faith evolves from the egocentricity of early childhood toward mature spiritual commitment in adulthood. However, emotional conflicts may cause developmental aberrations that lead to unhealthy and destructive forms of faith. Adults who fail to progress beyond the earlier stages are likely to have experienced more severe psychological traumas than those who function at higher stages.

Before elaborating each of the five stages in depth, a brief summary of the developmental phases will help to orient the reader.[1]

Stage 1: Egocentric Faith. People in stage one either magically identify with the omnipotent Other or attempt to appease a sadistic God that delights in punishing or abandoning them. Magical thinking, petitionary prayer and comfort seeking pervade the religious expression of religiously egocentric people. These people are highly unstable and use the religious arena to reenact their emotional traumas.

Stage 2: Dogmatic Faith. The religiously dogmatic are oriented toward earning God's love and approval. Intensely fearful of disappointing other people and God, they are compulsive in their conformance to religious codes. These people feel excessively guilty about their sexual and angry feelings, which they attempt to deny or suppress. Their harsh superegos and obsessive scrupulosity make them rigid and emotionally constricted. The religiosity of these people is characterized by self-denial, submission to authority and intolerance of diversity and ambiguity.

Stage 3: Transitional Faith. People in religious transition critically examine previously held beliefs and begin to reformulate their spiritual values and ideals. They renounce the tyranny of dogma for greater reliance on personal conscience. Until they become anchored in a self-chosen faith that is congruent with their emerging ideals, people in stage three may feel spiritually groundless and confused. Their religious expression may involve affiliational switching or experimentation with divergent faiths.

Stage 4: Reconstructed Faith. People in stage four are committed to a self-chosen faith that provides meaning, purpose and spiritual fulfillment. Their religious practice is guided by constructive, internalized morals and ideals. Although they are tolerant of religious diversity, residual needs to resolve ambiguities may lead these people toward a religious community that proposes definitive answers to their spiritual uncertainties.   If their ideological consolidation becomes impermeable to new spiritual insights, their faith will not undergo further progressive transformations.

Stage 5:   Transcendent Faith. Few people reach this level of spiritual evolution. Selfless devotion to goodness and truth enables these extraordinary individuals to experience a sense of community with people of all faiths and with God. They are passionately attuned to universal ideals and strive to fulfill the highest potentials in themselves and humankind.

NOTE

1. See Vicky Genia, "Religious Development: Synthesis and Reformulation," *Journal of Religion and Health* 29 (1990): 85-99.

Chapter 5

Stage 1: Egocentric Faith

At stage one, religion is rooted in fear and needs for comfort. Egocentric faith in adulthood is indicative of emotional disturbance related to early psychological trauma. As a result of childhood abuse or severe neglect, egocentric adults are incapable of forming stable, trusting and self-affirming bonds with others or with God.

The capacity for stable object relationships is established during the first three years of life. During this pre-Oedipal period the mother or primary caretaker who feeds, nurtures and cares for the infant becomes associated with the accompanying feelings of pleasure and satisfaction. However, because no one can always anticipate or intuit the infant's needs, and because infants and very young children have little tolerance for physical or emotional discomfort, the mother becomes associated with negative affects as well.

Under the dominion of the id impulses and the pleasure principle, infants wish to destroy the bearer of pain and distress. Yet they are utterly dependent on the caregiver for their survival. Therefore, they unconsciously preserve the symbiotic attachment by mentally "splitting" the caretaker into two separate images, one representing the "all-good" gratifying parent that the child idealizes and the other the "all-bad" frustrating parent that the child hates.

In other words, the very young child does not perceive the parent as the same person who sometimes pleases and sometimes distresses him. Instead, the child mentally experiences his pleasant and unpleasant interactions with the parent as separate relationships. This enables the child to keep the satisfying part of his relationship with the parent from being contaminated by his hateful feelings. Since the individual's course of development is established during the first few years of life, splitting in very early childhood is nature's provision for preserving and strengthening the parent-child bond.

In a sufficiently gratifying family matrix the child develops a secure attachment to the mother and feels safe and protected. Anchored to an attuned mother the young child gradually begins to integrate the separate images of her into a stable concept of someone who is generally affirming and trustworthy, but who sometimes frustrates him. As the child grows, emotionally satisfying relationships with both parents contribute to a positive and integrated sense of self and others.

When frustrating experiences are frequent and intense, the child fails to integrate the contradictory images. Instead, abused children overidealize their abusers. Contrary to what we might expect, children who are mistreated or severely neglected cling even more tenaciously to the abusive or unavailable parent. This dynamic occurs partly because even the most toxic parent provides some positive affirmation. Children starved for affection unceasingly hope for those rare moments when they will feel supported and loved.

In addition, children need to see their parents as good and trustworthy in order to feel protected and secure. Since infants and young children judge the world through the lens of the parent-child dyad, acknowledging the parent's guilt evokes terrifying visions of an unresponsive universe. Rather than face the overwhelming despair and hopelessness that accompany early disruption of this crucial developmental period, young children will blame themselves for the abuse. Denial of the parent's wrongdoing helps the child to manage overwhelming feelings of helplessness and preserve the illusion that the parent is good.

Memorializing an idealized image of the disparaging caregiver also helps the victimized child to sooth his fears of annihilation or abandonment. Mistreated children accumulate a reservoir of rage toward their persecutors. However, infants and very young children do not distinguish wishes from actions. Consequently, the abused child believes that his hateful thoughts will cause actual physical injury to the caregiver, thereby endangering his own survival. Fears of desertion or annihilation are exacerbated if the parent withdraws or retaliates whenever the child is assertive or demanding.

In order to mitigate their suffering, some severely mistreated children develop dissociative or delusional disorders. People who suffer extreme psychological hardship long to reexperience the sense of omnipotence that accompanies the symbiotic phase. Some cope with their pain by creating an illusory world where they feel that once again all things are possible. Others learn to protect themselves by becoming invisible or self-effacing. Still others cultivate an exaggerated sense of self-importance to help them feel invincible. All children who suffer devastating disappointments when their developing self is most fragile and vulnerable unconsciously retain a sense of entitlement to a responsive other. As a result, they become needy, manipulative adults who demand that others fill their insatiable needs for reassurance and affirmation.

Unfortunately, overreliance on idealization and other primitive defenses to sooth emotional fractures leads to deficits in forming integrated concepts of oneself and others. Adults who need to feel omnipotent cannot accept that people have human limitations. Instead, their reactions to others are under the dominion of their compelling needs for idealized attachments and mirroring. Tormented by a deep inner emptiness, people who were inadequately loved and nurtured relentlessly search for the perfect parent who will be infallibly attuned to their needs. They feel entitled to special treatment and become enraged when others fail to notice or appreciate them. People who disappoint them become the embodiment of the parents who abused and humiliated them and are vigorously attacked.

Because our self-images are partly formed through our interpersonal relationships, people who compulsively seek to merge themselves with infallible parent surrogates do not develop firm identities and have difficulty separating their own feelings from those of others. Their inability to maintain distinct boundaries between themselves and others, coupled with their highly erratic and tumultuous relationships, often leaves them feeling fragmented and at the mercy of forces beyond their control.[1]

When children's early attachments are unstable and harried, these patterns are carried forward into their adult religious practices and relationship to God.[2] Although people in stage one turn to religion for relief and comfort, their relationship to God becomes a reenactment of their traumatic relationships with their parents.

Because the religiously egocentric are extremely vulnerable to narcissistic injury, minor setbacks and disappointments lead them to experience God as a malevolent power who has intentionally and unjustly punished them. Feeling victimized by God is a reenactment of the sadomasochistic relationship with the primary caretakers. Religious individuals who were victims of their parents' rage and sadistic rampages assume that God also delights in humiliating and tormenting them. The egocentric's self-pity also reflects his feelings of entitlement to a responsive other.

During distressing times individuals who have received more than their fair share of childhood disappointments become acutely aware of feeling that God has cheated them. Indeed, they have been deprived of their birthright to be loved and protected. However, these people fear that their rageful recriminations will further incite God's retribution (as indeed happened with the abusive parent if the child dared to complain). The result would be gridlock and perpetual antagonism between themselves and God if not for massive efforts to restore God's goodness.

By convincing themselves that they are unlovable and unworthy of happiness, egocentrics can retain their faith in a universal source of goodness. Acceptance of their badness enables them to hope that love is still available. This defensive maneuver is facilitated by their fluid ego boundaries. The egocentric's disappointment in God is easily transformed into God's disappointment in her. Her despair is ameliorated by believing that God's grace will be forthcoming if she can mend her ways.

In exonerating God and the culpable parents by assuming the blame for their adversity, egocentrics organize their personalities around a core of self-contempt. That people raised in chaotic households tend to be impulsive and emotionally erratic serves to give credibility to their indictment of badness. Efforts to be perfect in order to be accepted are central to their religious observance. Ever hoping to be pleasing to God, the religiously egocentric may attempt to control their wildly fluctuating moods through scrupulous religious practice. Acquiescence to religious dogma may also help to quell overwhelming feelings of fragmentation and helplessness.

Evidence of early deprivation is also prevalent in the dynamics of prayer and moral reasoning at stage one. Egocentrics who pray normally do so to obtain special favors. Those with a modicum of hope for a more abundant life may use prayer as a prophylactic against further adversity and hardship. While efforts to beseech God for personal consideration are indicative of some inner disposition to trust a good object, the predominance of supplicatory prayer also reflects the magical thinking and persistent neediness that characterize people who were severely damaged in early development.

Deficits in superego development at this stage are most obvious in the egocentric's moral reasoning. Bereft of opportunities to internalize a consistent set of values, people in stage one judge right or wrong by expectations of reward or punishment.[3] Confession, if practiced, is used to avoid divine punishment. It is important to emphasize that the egocentric's admission of badness does not stem from realistic feelings of accountability or an inner sense of wrongdoing. Rather, feelings of self-hate are preferable to believing that God is ruthless and unresponsive to human need.

Notwithstanding that egocentrics are prone to submerge themselves in idealized attachments, they generally retain a rudimentary sense of self. They know that God and others have independent centers of initiative. However, some lose their psychological footing and envision themselves as an embodiment of the divine. This delusional, magical identification with God indicates a total collapse of boundaries between the self and others. The sense of oneness with the supreme being replicates the symbiotic union of mother and child. Others seek to restore the conditions of symbiosis by merging themselves with powerful, charismatic religious leaders.

Still other severely regressed egocentrics imagine that they are pursued by demonic forces.[4] These individuals reenact their antagonistic relationships with their childhood persecutors by engaging in illusory warfare against diabolical spirits. By projecting their family drama onto the cosmic plane and locating the badness in the devil, delusional egocentrics deny the unconscionable abuses that were inflicted on them by their parents.

I must emphasize that belief in opposing supernatural forces should not in itself be interpreted as a pathological sign. Confidence in God's ultimate triumph over Evil is central to the Judeo-Christian and Islamic traditions. Moreover, mystical experiences and transcendent encounters are not necessarily symptomatic of psychological disturbance. Whether or not a feeling of oneness with God is indicative of healthy self-transcendence or regression to symbiosis must be determined in light of the individual's developmental history and current level of psychosocial functioning.

Preoccupation with supernatural powers depicted as capricious, menacing personas that act with deliberate, malicious intent toward the believer suggests early abuse. Having been victimized as children by events beyond their control, people in stage one expect mistreatment. Thus, in their religious practice they attempt to appease a sadistic God that seems to delight in humiliating them. By appeasing God they hope to attain love and comfort.

This discussion should dispel temptations to criticize and judge the religiously egocentric. People who relate to others and to God as need-satisfying objects do not do so out of deliberate selfishness or insensitivity, but because of severe deprivations and mistreatment in infancy and early childhood. The egocentric has been repeatedly betrayed by the most significant people in his life, his parents. He is enraged not only at the abusive parent, but also, if raised in a two-parent household, at the nonabusive parent who failed to protect him. If the abusive parent was the father, his rage toward the mother for not protecting him contaminates the early bonding experience.

The plight of egocentric adults should spark our deepest compassion and understanding. Despite their yearning for a comforting and unambivalent attachment to God, their deep distrust and inner rage make them unable to experience God's availability and goodness. The individual in stage one unconsciously turns God into the parents who have failed him and then trembles before that projected, malevolent image.

In sum, people in stage one were severely emotionally damaged during their early development. As a result, their faith is child-like and self-centered. It is unlikely that they will mature spiritually without intensive psychotherapy to repair the effects of their psychological traumas.

NOTES

1. The primary resources for the preceding discussion are Gertrude Blanck and Rubin Blanck, *Ego Psychology: Theory and Practice* (New York: Columbia University Press, 1974); Otto Kernberg, *Borderline Conditions and Pathological Narcissism* (New York: Jason Aronson, 1985); and Margaret Mahler, Fred Pine, and Anni Bergman, *The Psychological Birth of the Human Infant* (New York: Basic Books, 1975).

2. Robert Lovinger, *Working with Religious Issues in Therapy* (New York: Jason Aronson, 1984); Ana-Maria Rizutto, *The Birth of the Living God* (Chicago: University of Chicago Press, 1979); Moshe Spero, ed., *Psychotherapy of the Religious Patient* (Springfield, Il.: Charles C. Thomas, 1985).

3. I have indicated points of convergence between my proposed stages and Lawrence Kohlberg's theory of moral development. For descriptions of Kohlberg's developmental stages, see Lawrence Kohlberg, *The Psychology of Moral Development* (San Francisco: Harper & Row, 1984); and Nathaniel Lande and Afton Slade, *Stages: Understanding How You Make Your Moral Decisions* (San Francisco: Harper & Row, 1979).

4. Robert Lovinger, "Religious Imagery in the Psychotherapy of a Borderline Patient," in *Psychotherapy of the Religious Patient*, ed. M. Spero, 181-207.

Chapter 6

Psychotherapy of the Egocentric Client

Evidence of the impoverished and tumultuous psychological climate of their families of origin pervades the spiritual expression of people in stage one. The egocentric is likely to exhibit many of the following characteristics:

- exhibits superstitious and magical thinking
- has erratic mood fluctuations
- fears abandonment
- feels shame or worthlessness
- seeks religion for comfort and emotional relief
- has low frustration tolerance and is impulse dominated
- relates to God as a need-satisfying object
- exhibits abrupt shifts in perceptions of self and others
- views the world as dangerous and threatening
- centers spiritual practice on appeasing a vengeful and intolerant God
- often fantasizes about power, greatness and perfection
- selectively attends to morbid aspects of religious ideology

ISSUES OF COMPETENCE

Owing to their family histories of domestic instability and emotional deprivation, egocentrics are vulnerable to a range of mental health problems, including anxiety, depression, personality disorders, addictions and compulsions, suicidal tendencies, impulsivity and poor interpersonal relationships. Their spiritual concerns cannot be disentangled from their childhood traumas and general emotional disequilibrium. The spiritually egocentric may be unwilling to acknowledge feelings of depression, anxiety or rage. Instead, they will symbolize these painful emotions through religious language and appear to be in a spiritual crisis.

However, for people in stage one, problems of faith are inextricably intertwined with their core psychological conflicts. Religious counselors who take their spiritual concerns at face value and fail to address the underlying pathology are unlikely to promote significant improvement in the counselee's outlook. On the other hand, secular therapists who undermine all religious belief and fail to acknowledge that disordered religiousness coexists with healthy spiritual striving devalue the client's experience and overlook valuable resources for emotional healing.

Religious and mental health professionals who counsel people with an egocentric spiritual orientation must be sufficiently proficient in developmental psychology and psychopathology to conceptualize the underlying trauma. Competence in diagnostic assessment and psychological intervention are also necessary prerequisites for treating people in stage one. Although the bonding with an empathic and nurturing counselor or religious community can be gratifying and temporarily reparative for the egocentric, emotional support alone fosters overidealization and dependency and reinforces splitting. Furthermore, their interpersonal relationships are contaminated by unconscious distortions and projections. The emotional healing needed for progressive faith transformation requires extensive and intensive examination of the client's mental processes.

THE THERAPEUTIC ALLIANCE

A safe, accepting and consistent therapeutic ambience is most essential to treating people in stage one. Even though a supportive environment alone is insufficient to produce permanent changes, a sense of connection to a nonjudgmental therapist provides the foundation for the exploratory work. Establishing a strong therapeutic alliance with the egocentric client is not an easy task and requires a great deal of patience and fortitude. Because egocentrics have experienced betrayal in their most significant relationships, their ability to trust others is seriously impaired. Conditioned to expect mistreatment, these clients repeatedly test the trustworthiness and sincerity of the therapist.

The therapist's equanimity can be severely challenged by the emotional neediness, manipulativeness and instability of people in stage one. The client in search of symbiotic attachment will initially tend to overidealize and placate the therapist. However, at the slightest disappointment these clients may become antagonistic and uncooperative. They may express their anger indirectly by becoming sullen and silent. The therapist should gently remind the withholding client of the task at hand, while respecting his or her need to titrate self-disclosure.

Rapid shifts in the egocentric's emotional state are likely to provoke complementary oscillations in the therapist's feelings toward the client, ranging from oversolicitous concern to hostility. The therapist must continually monitor his or her internal reactions and neither retaliate nor overindulge the client. It is important that the therapist accept the client's rage without becoming intimidated or emotionally distant. Calm acceptance of aggressive impulses communicates to the client that his or her feelings are not fundamentally bad and will not necessarily lead to catastrophic consequences. Nevertheless, professionals are not required to tolerate emotional abuse from their clients and must set clear limits with them. Encouraging the client to calmly examine, rather than act on, his or her destructive feelings serves to promote emotional integration and development of object constancy.

THE SELF-EFFACING EGOCENTRIC

The self-effacing egocentric experiences himself at the mercy of a capricious and unreliable God. Theologically astute stage one individuals can be quite adept in supporting their view of an erratic and fear-inspiring God through the scriptures of their faith. Since they selectively attend to specific passages that resonate with their inner experiences, their religious idiom provides important clues about their mental and emotional functioning.

The theological language used by egocentrics to express their core conflicts will vary depending upon their religious tradition. For example, sexually conflicted Jews or Moslems may be overscrupulous in their performance of purification rituals. By contrast, sexual guilt for the Protestant client may be unconsciously conveyed through fears of committing the unpardonable sin. Catholic clients may experience a sense of original sin that is unameliorated through confession and penance.

Therapists should not automatically assume that a client's belief in sin is indicative of a psychological disorder. A sense of human fallibility and an urge for wholeness through God's grace or covenant undergird Western faith traditions. Egocentrics are distinguished from mature believers by a pervasive and relentless shame identity that is unmitigated by confession or rituals for expiation.

The religious imagery of self-effacing clients also mirrors the unstable nature of their attachments. Their highly charged ambivalent feelings may be split into two divine figures with opposing attributes. Fear and hatred of the abusive caregiver(s) and the humiliated self are externalized and demonified into a supernatural being of unlimited evil. The wished-for parent is deified and brought to its highest splendor in the purified God representation.

The egocentric's fear of fragmentation may also find religious expression. Preoccupation with apocalyptic imagery suggests that the client has projected his internal chaos and poorly regulated aggression onto the cosmic plane. The graphic portrayal of cataclysmic events and imminent world destruction in the New Testament's Book of Revelation may personify for Christian clients disruption of the symbiotic bond and fear of annihilation. For Jewish clients the gruesome accounts of religious wars in the Old Testament may serve to express unconscious horrors.

In sum, formative experiences coalesce with frightening religious stories and myths, leaving the self-effacing believer feeling threatened from within and without.

The religious therapist may be tempted to reassure the client by quoting scriptural passages that convey God's accessibility and responsiveness to human need. The irreligious therapist, on the other hand, may try to liberate the client from his divine tormentor by cajoling him into believing that God is an illusion. Both approaches trivialize the client's experience. The egocentric client has little in his or her psychological repertoire from which to conceptualize a benevolent or loving deity. Since disordered religiousness is not the cause, but the consequence of psychological trauma, obliteration of religious belief is not a cure for psychic pain.

If introduced prematurely, direct religious teaching can create a painful state of cognitive dissonance. The client will feel as if the therapist is imposing a view of reality that is incongruent with his or her inner experience. Belief in a wrathful God is deeply ingrained in the egocentric's emotional set. Moreover, the sense of worthlessness that has been unconsciously instilled from early childhood by deprecatory caregivers renders the client incapable of accepting God's love. Theological evidence of God's goodness to humankind serves not to salve the wounded spirit of the self-debasing believer, but to further entrench him in self-contempt and despair. If the egocentric can be persuaded that love is available in the universe, he will be equally convinced that he is not getting it because he is unlovable. The healing of deep emotional wounds is necessary before a self-affirming faith can flourish. In order to accomplish this difficult task, the client's trust must be gently nurtured through a consistent and reliable therapeutic relationship.

I am not suggesting that it is never appropriate to use religious teachings in therapy, only that it is unlikely to be effective in its initial phases. At later stages of the therapy process, judicious use of relevant spiritual teachings with clients who are receptive to this approach can enhance and progress the psychological work. However, exploratory work must precede direct attempts to reformulate the client's theology.

THE NARCISSISTIC EGOCENTRIC

The descriptive "narcissistic egocentric" may seem tautological. However, the terms are not synonymous. Egocentrics are driven by their needs and insecurities, but are not necessarily egotistical. The narcissistically religious compose a sub-group of people in the egocentric stage who are characterized by an expanded sense of self-importance. On the surface they appear calm, confident and self-assured. Their underlying sense of unworthiness and unlovability is covered by a thick layer of grandiosity.

The self-inflated religious client is convinced that he or she has been "called" by God for special service or "chosen" for God's unique mission. However, he or she lacks the self-discipline, moral stamina and deep compassion for others that characterize spiritual leaders who are genuinely dedicated to religious service. The narcissistically religious seek positions of religious authority for self-enhancement, rather than for service to God. Their spiritual life serves their exaggerated need for recognition and adulation.

In contrast to the typically chaotic and grossly neglectful parenting of the self-effacing egocentric, the personal histories of narcissistic types reveal that many were pampered and overindulged. However, the overindulgent caretakers related to the child not as a separate person, but as an extension of themselves. These parents need an extraordinary child to compensate for their own failures and inadequacies. In the process of transferring their own ambitions onto the child, the caregivers stifle the child's uniqueness and individuality.

Children who develop narcissistic personalities were deflated and deprecated for their failure to mirror the caregiver's lofty expectations. As a result, emotional bonding became associated with engulfment and humiliation. They learned that their human limitations and weaknesses make them unlovable and unwanted. If the child has special talents, he may suppress his spontaneity and individuality and cultivate those qualities that are favored by the parents. Less gifted children may retreat to an illusory aggrandized self to sustain their self-esteem. Eventually, in either case, the child identifies with this "false self" and experiences intolerable shame when he fails to realize his ambitions of greatness.

Unlike the self-effacing type, who fears abandonment, the narcissistic individual's greatest fear is vulnerability. Since he associates dependency with loss of identity, the narcissistic type overidentifies with his inflated sense of himself and becomes compulsively self-reliant. He does not form stable attachments and abruptly withdraws his emotional energy from people who do not reinforce his exaggerated feelings of self-importance.

Because religious leaders are exalted in the eyes of their followers, some narcissistic personalities gravitate toward religion. While claiming to be called by God, the narcissistic spiritual leader secretly deifies himself and promotes his own glorification. Unconsciously, he has absorbed God into his grandiose self and relies on his own sense of omnipotence. His identification with God, coupled with his insatiable need for affirmation and admiration, lead him to feel entitled to the unwavering devotion of his followers.

People who use religion for self-enhancement are alienated from themselves, others and God. Without spiritual nourishment and human connection they become hungry and depleted. However, since narcissistic personalities expect humiliation and condemnation for normal human longings, they desperately cling to their armor of grandiosity.

The narcissistically religious will not seek help unless severe setbacks shatter the sustaining admired self. Loss of recognition is experienced as unbearable humiliation and leads to catastrophic loss of self-esteem. In working with narcissistic clients, empathy is the most important therapeutic skill and the most difficult to sustain because of their devaluative stance toward helpers. The client's contemptuous attitude toward caregivers reflects not only his unacknowledged rage toward his parents, but also a displacement of the intolerance that he feels toward himself for his neediness and deficiencies. Before the therapy can progress, the client must be assured that he will not be ridiculed.

The royal road to the client's "true self" is the long and tortuous path of empathic mirroring. Secular therapists who directly challenge the narcissist's belief in his chosen status will be swiftly abandoned. Exhortations to be realistic and reasonable only serve to enrage the client or make him more despondent.

The religious therapist who convicts the self-inflated client of committing the sin of pride will also incite his rage or cause him to feel degraded and demoralized. The narcissistic personality cannot tolerate a sense of himself as a sinner in need of forgiveness. However, his self-exaltation and need to be infallible are not willful self-idolatry or disobedience to God, but an unconscious maneuver to compensate for deficits in self-regulation resulting from early empathic failures. The individual equates spiritual humility with the humiliations of childhood. The original narcissistic injury must be healed before he can allow himself to be humble.

The therapist should begin by acknowledging and appreciating how difficult it is for the client to seek help. Feeling understood and accepted disarms the client's need to appear infallible. Acknowledging his disillusionment and neediness is the first step toward helping him to tolerate his human longings and vulnerabilities.

The relationship with an empathically attuned therapist gradually erodes the compulsion to maintain an aggrandized self. As the client's individuality is nurtured through the therapeutic partnership, he learns that God, too, can endure the hated and unacceptable parts of himself.

A spiritual transformation occurs as the parental projections are dislodged and the client experiences God as without judgment or expectation. As his faith develops, he loses his need to be in a position of superiority. A confluence of spiritual and psychological regeneration and integration enables the individual to appreciate his talents and accomplishments, while humbly accepting his limitations and liabilities. Fear of his dependency needs subsides, and the client develops affectionate ties to the religious community, significant others and God.[1]

THE DELUSIONAL EGOCENTRIC

The delusional egocentric creates and enters an esoteric world of angels and demons. Visual and auditory hallucinations may augment his frightening internal escapades.

Notwithstanding that there are distinct differences between self-effacing and narcissistic egocentrics, both types are generally capable of distinguishing reality from fantasy and can engage in normal interpersonal discourse. Despite his self-deification, the narcissistic individual knows that he is not God. However, severely regressed narcissistic personalities may be convinced that they are endowed with transcendent qualities and magical powers. This delusional identification with the Divine is a deranged form of religiosity that indicates serious psychopathology.

Self-effacing religiosity can also be twisted to extremes. As mentioned previously, self-effacing egocentrics are prone to dwell on morbid thoughts. Yet they rarely report actual encounters with diabolical beings. By contrast, the delusional egocentric with self-debasing tendencies feels himself submerged in a frightening world of persecutory evil spirits. His intolerable self-hatred, fear of annihilation and rage toward his childhood persecutors are personified in the form of ghosts or devils who relentlessly pursue and torment him. Feelings of powerlessness against those who abused him, combined with internal representations of adults who failed to protect him, may lead the delusional client to envision God as a weak and passive figure who succumbs to the forces of evil. A particularly ominous dynamic occurs when the client feels intrapsychically merged with the caretaker who tormented him and consequently identifies himself as a powerful, malevolent force.

In each of these examples the psychotic process has become attached to religious symbols. Clients who present with religious delusions or extremely disordered thinking should be immediately referred for a thorough psychiatric evaluation, preferably in a hospital. Delusional egocentrics may be a danger to themselves or others and should initially be treated in an inpatient setting. Antipsychotic medications may ameliorate the frightening delusions and help restore more logical thinking.

Once the patient is stabilized, ongoing psychological treatment on an outpatient basis should be initiated. With severely disturbed clients an "existential-phenomenological" approach[2] may be more successful than an analytic-interpretive one.

Therapists who treat delusional patients must be competent in treating psychotic and severe personality disorders. The patient's deranged religiosity is inseparable from his broader psychological impairment. Since psychotrophic medications may be indicated to manage thought and mood disturbances, collaboration with a psychiatrist is strongly recommended.

ANGER AND FORGIVENESS

Most religious traditions urge their adherents to forgive those who have willfully wronged them. Religious therapists who view the egocentric's bitterness as an insurmountable obstacle to cultivating an attitude of compassion and forgiveness may discourage expression of angry feelings. However, insisting that patients forgive their abusive childhood caretakers before fully acknowledging and working through their rage puts the cart before the horse.

The self-pity and resentment that consume people in stage one are not the direct cause of their emotional and spiritual disturbances, but the consequences of excessive psychological hardship. Therapists that foist forgiveness by reminding the client of the caregiver's positive qualities, while minimizing or rationalizing the abuse, distort the religious imperative to forgive. A hasty pardon before the client fully absorbs and integrates the violations inflicted on his personhood reinforces denial and halts progress toward establishing realistic concepts of the self and others.

Religious counselors that encourage women to remain in marriages with abusive husbands not only distort religious imperatives to forgive, but also promote revictimization. Many women unconsciously reenact their childhood abuse by becoming involved with men who mistreat them. Thus, the religious professional who advises a woman to stay in a destructive marriage not only sanctions exploitation, but also serves to inflict more emotional damage on the woman's already abused self. Allowing oneself to be repeatedly disparaged is not in the service of God, but constitutes religiously sanctioned masochism.

The above comments are intended not to undermine efforts to promote a more forgiving and empathic outlook, but to establish their appropriate place in the clinical work. Genuine forgiveness requires a realistic assessment of wrongdoing followed by a conscious decision to release the transgressor from further obligation. The client whose attachments are distorted by projections and idealizations and dominated by need gratification lacks the emotional autonomy and psychological maturity to experience true compassion and understanding.

It might be helpful to conceptualize the path to forgiveness as a four-step process.

1. *Encourage the client to acknowledge his or her anger.* Premature forgiveness inhibits the emotional healing that results from confronting and working through the rage of victimization. The client should be assisted in connecting his or her diffuse anger to its source, the early caretakers. To accomplish this task, the therapist must accept the client's hostile feelings without judgment.

2. *Normalize the client's rage.* Although therapists do not condone destructive behaviors, they must help clients understand that their resentments are legitimate reactions to mistreatment. Clients may also need permission to ventilate their rage toward God without fear of retaliation. People in stage one are envious of those with healthier families and feel cheated of their birthright to be loved and nurtured. These feelings must be acknowledged and not labeled as sinful.

3. *Help the client grieve.* People who felt unloved by their parents carry a reservoir of hurt and sadness. After the client has acknowledged and appropriately expressed his or her angry feelings, a process of grieving ensues. The client grieves many losses: loss of a happy childhood, loss of the hope that his or her parents will make up for past deprivations, loss of aggrandized self-impressions and loss of the belief in magical solutions to life's problems.

Therapeutic techniques that may facilitate the grief work include journal writing, guided imagery and bibliotherapy. The empty-chair technique can help clients express feelings to parents without fear of reprisal. I sometimes have clients write letters to the offending parent and read them to me during the therapy hour. Knowing that the letter will not be mailed allows the client to elaborate his or her thoughts and feelings without censorship. Some clients chose to mail an edited version of the letter.

These exercises may release very powerful and intense emotions. In conducting grief work the therapist must carefully monitor the timing and pacing to ensure that the client is not overwhelmed.

4. *Promote forgiveness.* Even though traditional psychotherapy does not usually directly address the issue of forgiveness, secular therapists must not overlook the importance of this step for religiously committed clients.

As a result of working through their rage and disappointment, clients establish more realistic concepts of themselves and others. They understand that they were not abused or neglected because they were bad or unloveable, but were simply victims of circumstances beyond their control. Since they no longer cling to idealized images of the wished-for parents or fear the sadistic and humiliating images, these clients can forgive their parents for being emotionally depleted and immature people who were incapable of adequately nurturing their children.

Therapists as well as clients should keep in mind that forgiveness is not an all-or-nothing phenomenon, but a process that occurs over time. After the client completes a phase of the work, other painful memories may suddenly be recalled that rekindle intense feelings of resentment or sadness. Clients may progress and regress through the anger grief forgiveness sequence many times throughout the course of therapy.

Two additional points on the topic of forgiveness should be mentioned. First, *forgiveness is not exoneration.* The client who chooses to forgive makes a conscious decision to pardon someone who has inflicted harm to himself or herself. This does not mean that the violator is absolved of his or her actions or that all feelings of anger have dissipated. The abuser remains accountable to God for his or her infractions. However, through forgiveness, the victim relinquishes entitlement to retaliation or restitution and tempers anger with compassion.

Second, *forgiveness is not reconciliation.* Forgiveness is not an obligation to remain in an abusive relationship. Although forgiveness may be a first step in a conciliatory process, it need not necessarily lead to reconciliation. In order to reestablish the relationship the offender must acknowledge wrongdoing and desist behaviors that are damaging and reprehensible. If the abuser is unwilling to change, the client may rightfully refuse to have further contact with him or her.

PRAYER FOR INNER HEALING

Christian therapists who conduct "Biblically informed" therapy integrate spiritual approaches with traditional psychotherapeutic methods. Prayer for inner healing combines intercessory prayer with guided imagery of Jesus to promote healing of psychological trauma. Although this technique has attracted enthusiastic proponents, inner healing has also received scathing criticism. While prayer can be a powerful force in the service of psychospiritual healing, the limitations and potential iatrogenic effects of this approach with egocentric clients should be carefully considered.

First, prayer can be used for the wrong reasons. Therapists may feel threatened and repelled by their clients' histories of parental exploitation, some of which shatter our basic assumptions about the innocence of children and the sanctity of the family. Helpers also experience indignation, feelings of helplessness, guilt and grief when listening to gruesome accounts of sexual abuse or abject cruelty by childhood caretakers. These uncomfortable feelings may prompt the therapist to attempt a quick healing.

When employing inner healing techniques, the therapist must be attuned to his or her motives, client readiness and appropriate timing. Therapists that use prayer defensively turn away from the suffering of their clients. This misuse of inner healing not only impedes the client's recovery, but also further entrenches his or her devalued sense of self. Dr. Siang-Yang Tan, a Christian psychologist, warns that

prayer can be misused or abused. Both the client as well as the therapist may at times resort to prayer as an avoidance of difficult issues that have emerged in the therapy. A clinically sensitive and competent therapist will do some self-evaluation of motives for using prayer and seek consultation and supervision from Christian professional colleagues where necessary.[3]

A second caution relates to the client's fragmented perceptions of self and others. The egocentric's images of God are grossly distorted by unconscious projections. Guided imagery may raise anxiety to intolerable levels in clients who tremble before tyrannical or vengeful God representations. Furthermore, receptivity to God's healing power requires some attenuation, if not dissolution, of the client's contemptuous or grandiose self-perceptions.

Tan reminds us that

> A Christian client who is struggling with bitterness or resentment toward God
> . . . may not be ready for or receptive to direct prayer at the present time. He
> or she may be more open to the use of prayer in later sessions after some of
> his or her feelings and struggles have been worked through with the patient and
> skillful help of the Christian therapist who shows acceptance and understanding
> of the client.[4]

Finally, if initiated too early in the therapy, use of inner healing may foster overdependency on the therapist and discourage self-responsibility. Since egocentrics are prone to seek idealized attachments and magical solutions as substitutes for constructive problem-solving, these methods may encourage the client to use God and the therapist as need-gratifying objects. Moreover, if immediate results are not attained, the subsequent disillusionment may overwhelm the client or undermine the treatment.

In working with people in stage one, therapists must be careful not to collude with them to expect magical elimination of psychic pain. Whereas prayer may spark hope and optimism, it will not wash away the indelible marks of degradation.

With appropriate caution, prayer for inner healing may have powerful therapeutic effects when facilitated by a sensitive therapist who sees beyond the brokenness and pain and appreciates the genuine spiritual thrust of the individual. The following guidelines are offered to maximize positive results.

1. Therapists have an ethical responsibility not to practice outside their areas of competence. Use of inner healing methods without appropriate training and supervision constitutes an ethical violation. Because traditional counseling and psychology programs rarely include preparation for addressing psychospiritual issues in treatment, secular therapists who wish to incorporate spiritual methods into their repertoires must seek additional training.

2. The therapist must have a clear rationale for incorporating prayer into the clinical work and be able to articulate this to the client. Even though specific outcomes cannot always be reliably predicted, the client and the clinician should agree on the purposes for which the interventions are intended.

3. The client must be receptive to the use of spiritual interventions and far enough along in the therapy to have hope for recovery and faith in God as a "good object." Hope and faith require a foundation of basic trust. Clients who

continually test the trustworthiness and sincerity of the therapist need more time to establish a positive therapeutic alliance.

4. Clients and therapists must guard against unreasonable expectations, yet not place limits on God's power. The ultimate challenge is to be realistic and at the same time receptive to the miraculous and the unexpected.

5. Clients should be encouraged to participate fully in their recovery and to view inner healing as a collaboration among the client, the therapist and God. Those who perceive themselves as passive recipients of special interventions will remain stunted in their psychospiritual development.

6. Unlike mainstream clinical techniques, the effectiveness of spiritual interventions is presumed to depend primarily on God's healing power, not on the skillfulness of the therapist. Therefore, the therapist's clinical expertise must be augmented with a strong personal faith. Skeptical or spiritually troubled practitioners should not initiate these procedures until their own issues of faith have been sufficiently resolved.

SUDDEN CONVERSIONS

Secular therapists in particular may be appalled by the egocentric's sudden conversion to a "born again" faith. However, for people in stage one, conversion is an indication that God has become approachable. The ability to trust in a good object and experience a stable, positive relationship with Jesus is a monumental step in the client's psychospiritual development. The outpouring of the human heart that occurs during conversions indicates that the egocentric's self-effacing or grandiose self-perceptions have significantly eroded.

The client's receptivity to God's love and goodness and his or her enthusiastic participation in a religious community are testimony to the success of the therapy. Remember that our most assiduous efforts are not likely to catapult the egocentric into stage five. Although we might prefer that clients bypass the dogmatic stage, it is an important stepping stone along the developmental pathway to mature faith. Authoritarian religious groups that temper dogmatism with genuine love and commitment provide new converts with a secure spiritual base and a temporary refuge.

Therapists may be legitimately concerned about the egocentric client who joins a highly intrusive and demanding religious group. However, direct attempts to extricate the client from an authoritarian group further undermine his or her autonomy and self-responsibility. Unless his or her involvement is life-threatening, the clinician must allow the client to remain in the victim role until he or she works through the unconscious need to be revictimized. As with clients who become entangled in masochistic interpersonal relationships, therapeutic neutrality and understanding must be maintained with those who join pernicious religious communities. With patience and skillful interpretations the client will eventually understand his or her involvement in destructive religious groups as an unconscious reenactment of childhood abuse.

My clinical work with a young man whom I will call Brian illustrates how faith can be poisoned by negative emotional experiences in child hood. Brian is typical of someone in stage one. This case study is presented in detail in the next chapter to help the reader better understand the dynamics of egocentric religiosity.

NOTES

1. The psychotherapuetic treatment of a narcissistic religious client is presented in James Klieger, "Emerging from the 'Dark Night of the Soul': Healing the False Self in a Narcissistically Vulnerable Minister," *Psychoanalytic Psychology* 7 (1990): 211-224.

2. A thorough review of a clinician's work with a delusional egocentric can be found in David Bradford, "A Therapy of Religious Imagery for Paranoid Schizophrenic Psychosis," in *Psychotherapy of the Religious Patient*, ed. M. Spero (Springfield, Il.: Charles C. Thomas, 1985), 154-180.

3. Siang-Yang Tan, "Explicit Integration in Psychotherapy" (paper presented at the International Congress on Christian Counseling, Counseling and Spirituality Track, Atlanta, November 1988), 6.

4. Ibid., 7.

Chapter 7

The Case of Brian: God of Wrath

Brian is a nineteen-year-old college student who is intellectually bright, musically talented and socially withdrawn. He attends classes regularly and punctually and participates in musical performances, but maintains only superficial contact with his peers. During his free time he prefers solitary activities such as listening to music or watching TV. In addition to being socially estranged, Brian exhibits chronic anxiety, mild depression and an eccentric personality style characterized by lack of vitality and zest. His emotional detachment covers an underlying hypersensitivity to criticism and an intense fear of rejection.

During his freshman year Brian was referred for counseling after experiencing a severe anxiety attack during an exam. Initially, Brian was resistant to exploring personal issues and insisted that his only problem was stress related to academic and other external demands. He provided a sketchy psychosocial history and saw little purpose in discussing issues not directly related to his immediate concerns.

Despite his dread of self-disclosure Brian was prompt and consistent in keeping his weekly appointments. At first he maintained very little eye contact and was extremely reluctant to communicate his thoughts and feelings. He spent most of the hour presenting monologues about

Reprinted, with changes, from *Journal of Religion and Health* 31 (1992): 317-326. Copyright 1992 by Institutes of Religion and Health. Reprinted by permission of Plenum Publishing Corp.

his weekly activities, punctuated by long silences. For example, during one session Brian provided a detailed description of how he planned to do his laundry later that afternoon. After he ran out of things to say, Brian became silent, stared at some object in the room and appeared oblivious to my presence. When I inquired about his thoughts, Brian frequently answered that he was concentrating on a piece of music or some detail in the surroundings such as the sound of a bird outside the window, an airplane flying overhead or a spot on the ceiling.

As therapy progressed, Brian became more at ease and spontaneously presented memories of dreams and childhood events. However, he discussed these experiences in a detached and fragmented manner and recoiled from any encouragement to explore the material. At other times he communicated his personal history metaphorically through discussions about literature, music or movies. By the end of his sophomore year a clinical profile began to take form. Brian was terrified of his narcissistic, eccentric and emotionally volatile father. His mother was nurturing and supportive, but her extreme passivity and vulnerability to major depressive episodes did not enable her to provide a secure emotional foundation for Brian.

His parents were in their late thirties when Brian was born. Because he was born with a congenital defect, the exact nature of which Brian refused to disclose, they decided against having more children. The deformity is not outwardly visible, and Brian simply referred to his disfigurement as "it." When I commented that the issue appeared not to have been "discussed" in the family, Brian replied that yes, indeed, "disgust" was the correct word to describe "it." Obviously, the physical defect continued to exert a tremendous negative impact on his already fragile self-esteem.

Before Brian was born, his father had been pastor of a Christian fundamentalist church. However, his education in philosophy and history contributed to a liberal theological orientation that made him unpopular with his highly conservative congregation. Devastated by the rejection of his colleagues and congregation members, he renounced his faith and became a history professor at a local college.

Brian's father is a tyrannical, volatile man who expects perfection and absolute obedience from his son. As a child Brian learned that the slightest irritation was likely to provoke his father's rage, followed by long, angry silences. Disinclined to show affection, Brian's father rarely expressed love or appreciation. Yet he was quick to ridicule Brian for no apparent reason.

Brian's mother, on the other hand, is a kind, but passive, woman who was taught to be submissive and compliant. As a result, she did not protect Brian from his father's sadistic rampages. She admitted to Brian that she was tremendously disappointed by his father's decision to leave the religious profession, but she never voiced these feelings directly to her husband. Instead, she suffered silently and experienced severe, and at times incapacitating, episodes of depression. Brian's mother remained affiliated with the fundamentalist church, and when her mood was stable, she was socially active, energetic and cheerful. Brian accompanied his mother to church until his parents separated.

When Brian was in his early teens, his parents divorced. He was never informed of their reasons for dissolving the marriage. Following the divorce Brian's mother moved into a small apartment in a nearby town. Brian remained in the family home with his father, but maintained frequent contact with his mother. Neither parent remarried, although Brian's father has dated several women since the divorce.

As the only child of a condescending and deprecating father and a depressed and inadequate mother, Brian became shy, withdrawn and detached. His social reticence and emotional insulation prevented him from developing self-confirming interactions with his peers, thereby intensifying his loneliness and sense of inadequacy. Feeling alienated and alone, he immersed himself in music and literature, which provided him with vicarious emotional and social experiences. Development of his gifted intelligence and identification with fictional characters enabled Brian to form a rudimentary, but fragile, sense of self. This fragility is best illustrated by his memory of looking into a mirror and feeling surprised that "I am me." The dissociative quality of his self experience reveals his vulnerability to fragmentation.

Since Brian feels compelled to become the perfect son that he hopes his father can accept, he suppresses the parts of himself that are incongruent with his father's expectations. His compulsive perfectionism gives him a sense of control that helps him to maintain a tenuous emotional equilibrium. However, the core of self-contempt that lurks beneath the false self leads him to feel shame and worthlessness at the slightest sign of criticism or disapproval.

Although Brian no longer participates in formal religion, he experiences an intense inner struggle with God that directly parallels his unconscious conflicts with his father. This transference is perhaps facilitated by the fact that his father was a clergyman. Brian's religious imagery is replete with characteristics of his father. However, his God images contain qualities of his mother as well. Brian's level of spiritual development is best exemplified by two religious themes that emerged in the therapy.

The first centers on Brian's memory of his reactions to a religious painting in his grandmother's home. When Brian was a young child, he and his mother frequently spent weekends in the country with his grandmother. During these visits Brian sometimes spent hours sitting by himself in the living room staring at the painting.

In the painting Jesus, surrounded by a group of admiring children, is holding a young boy on his lap. From Brian's vantage point Jesus seemed to be looking not at the children in the painting, but at him sitting on the couch. The expression on Jesus' face appeared to Brian to convey both "grace and wrath." Brian remembered, "I *felt* only the wrath but I *knew* the grace was there." As he stared at the painting, he contained his mounting fear by believing that "if I become good, God will accept His son." For Brian, goodness denotes perfection.

The Jesus of "wrath and grace" represents Brian's splitting of highly contradictory images of, and associated feelings toward, his father. On the one hand, he yearns for the recognition and affirmation of a compassionate father. On the other hand, he is enraged at and unconsciously wishes to destroy the sadistic father who terrifies him. The angry Jesus is partly a projection of his own anger toward an unfair father who humiliates him. Unable to allow his rage into conscious awareness, Brian transfers the conflict with his father onto God, whom he experiences as condemning him. Furthermore, he believes that God's condemnation is justified. Feeling overwhelmed with guilt, Brian confesses that he "lies about everything."

On one level his admission of guilt accurately depicts his failure to be true to himself. He suppresses his own feelings and wishes and molds himself into whatever he thinks will please his father. He states, "I am not me but what I made myself become." Brian's judgment of himself also indicates how thoroughly he has internalized his father's deprecating attitude toward him. Unappreciated by his father, he now devalues himself.

On a deeper level Brian's shame is a defensive maneuver in which he exonerates his father by blaming himself for the abuse. This enables Brian to avoid not only the rage that he feels toward his father, but also the devastating recognition of his father's need to demoralize him in order to compensate for his own feelings of powerlessness and inferiority.

By blaming himself for his father's "wrath" and striving to become the perfect son, Brian can continue to fantasize that his father will one day embrace him with his "grace." In the meanwhile he remains on the periphery, waiting to become his father's special child. Brian's total acceptance of his badness helps him retain the hope that there is love available in both his father and God. He believes that he is not getting that love because he himself is unworthy.

The second theme that serves to underscore the egocentric quality of his faith concerns Brian's strategy for coping with his congenital defect. This disfiguration, more than anything else, threatens his hope for ever receiving love. As Brian states, "This flaw is the key to everything."

Firmly believing that God will not accept him until he is indefectible, Brian further reasons that God must make it possible for him to eliminate his deformity. Otherwise, he argues, reconciliation would be unattainable, thereby implying that God is cruel and unjust. Since God cannot be bad, Brian concludes that his handicap is a "test" from God. He is determined to "prove God's goodness" through the healing of his disfigurement.

Brian prays intently for God to transform him into a "normal person." He is especially prone to anticipate "the miracle" on special days such as his birthday. Each time the "miracle doesn't happen," Brian becomes extremely agitated and self-contemptuous. He turns his disappointment in God into God's disappointment in him. Deeply ashamed of his body, Brian frantically attempts to "discover the laws of the universe" that will enable him to heal himself. His preoccupation with science fiction supports his belief in the possibility of accomplishing this feat.

Several features of this drama underscore the egocentricity of Brian's faith. First, his supplications illustrate the magical thinking and orientation to need gratification that characterize the prayers of religiously egocentric people. Second, the obsessive quality of his concern with his physical appearance indicates an extreme vulnerability to narcissistic injury. For Brian, any imperfection revivifies his feelings of self-hate, which stem from early disconfirmation of his sense of self-worth. Finally, his lack of clear differentiation between himself and God is exemplified here. Disappointed by God's failure to perform the miracle, he magically identifies with God's omnipotence and attempts to heal himself.

Brian's presumption that he is the center of God's volition and interest is another salient indicator of the primitive quality of his thinking. His images portray only dyadically fused involvements. No mention is made of other people with the exception of the admiring children in the painting, who passively observe the father figure holding the privileged child. He feels himself to be a despicable creature, inextricably bound to a sadistic God who delights in humiliating him. His hope is to banish his negative features in order to merge with God's "perfect goodness." Failing in this attempt he elaborates his own omnipotence and assumes the capacity to control the forces of the universe.

Brian's obsession with creating a faultless self is not only a hope for attaining the affections of the wished-for father, but also a strategy for containing his disorganized and frightening emotions and experiencing a sense of control. In addition, by focusing his efforts on the one aspect of himself that he cannot change, he avoids the terrible discovery that his search for the affirming father is futile. The hope of transforming himself also protects him from being totally submerged in self-hate.

Analysis of Brian's images and associations also illustrates how religious ideology can be absorbed into the pathological process and become the vehicle for expressing disordered mental states. Christian theology teaches that through faith in Christ, who is "without blemish" (1 Peter 1:19), the sinner is absolved of guilt. Yet this portrayal of Christ has no reality for Brian. He can only envision the wrathful deity that he secretly despises. In a massive effort to deny his rage, Brian endeavors to restore God's goodness through his own flawlessness. This inversion of Christian doctrine further demonstrates his fluid sense of himself and the permeability of his boundaries. Remnants of the religious education that Brian received at his mother's fundamentalist church also reinforce his vision of a vengeful God who demands sinlessness and torments the unrighteous.

On rare occasions during our work Brian admitted that he felt cheated by God. His envy of others with loving families was poignant during these brief revelations. I believe that this admission was possible because his terrifying God images were tempered by maternal projections. Brian's gratifying experiences with his mother, and perhaps his grandmother as well, enabled him to develop some capacity to tolerate ambivalent feelings.

Brian's ability to imagine Jesus as tender and compassionate reflects not only a wish for the loving father, but also the mother's nurturing during her more stable periods. As the young Brian gazed at the painting, he might have been comforted by memories of being held by his mother. However, because she was powerless to protect him from his father's violent moods, her arms of "grace," although momentarily soothing, could not shield him from his father's "wrath."

Desperately in need of soothing and comfort, Brian's faith is very child-like. His spiritual vision is narrow and egocentric. God is the personification of his personal family trauma. His only spiritual goal is to become God's favored child. He experiences no sense of spiritual connection or community.

Brian's identification with both the child in Jesus' lap and the child on the couch outside the circle of children personifies his central conflict. He both desires and fears affection and attachment. His father's unpredictable rages and his mother's depressive withdrawals created a frightening and confusing world for Brian. His parents' failure to securely anchor him in stable and predominantly gratifying attachments left him without the foundation of basic trust that is necessary for developing mature relationships with others and with God. Although Brian is aware of the presence of people in his environment, he remains emotionally detached from them. While protecting him from rejection and humiliation, his disconnection creates an inner world of emptiness, despair and longing.

Until Brian fully confronts his pain and rage, he will be incapable of developing a healthy religious outlook that is uncontaminated by his emotional conflicts. At present Brian can neither separate himself from the role his father has cast for him nor differentiate his father from God. Thus, he unceasingly attempts to appease a frightening, tyrannical God who demands perfection. This impossible task keeps him hypervigilant, guarded and chronically depressed. His only relief is the thread of hope for attaining the love and comfort that has been denied him.

Chapter 8

Stage 2: Dogmatic Faith

William James described two distinct, but interrelated, facets of spiritual conviction:

first, the present incompleteness or wrongness, the "sin" which he is eager to escape from; and, second, the positive ideal which he longs to compass. Now with most of us the sense of our present wrongdoing is a far more distinct piece of our consciousness than is the imagination of any positive ideal we can aim at.[1]

Quoting Edwin Starbuck, James agrees that the spiritual striving of most believers is " 'a process of struggling away from sin rather than a striving towards righteousness.' "[2] This " 'struggling away from sin' " describes the spiritual motivation of those in the dogmatic stage.

By rooting religion in the Oedipal struggle and the necessity for instinctual renunciation, Sigmund Freud also emphasized the guilt aspects of religion. According to Freud, children between the ages of three and five have strong sexual desires for the parent of the opposite sex. Their wish for exclusive possession of the opposite-sex parent leads them to fantasize about doing away with the same-sex parent. As a result of strong taboos against incestuous passions, children resolve the complex by relinquishing the obsession with the parent of the opposite sex and identifying with the parent of the same sex. This resolution culminates in the formation of a personal conscience or superego. By internalizing social prohibitions individuals become self-regulating and morally responsible. Failure to conform to the ideals of the superego results in feelings of anxiety and guilt. Freud believed that religion was devised to assist the superego in constraining the prurient and violent urges of ordinary people.[3]

Unfortunately, families and social groups that overemphasize renunciation of sexual and aggressive feelings create neurotic individuals who are afraid of their normal human emotions. Since a sin-focused religiosity reverberates with their harsh superegos, many neurotics are drawn to oppressive and demanding religious groups.

Moral anxiety and trusted authority play a prominent role in the faith of school-age children. Subordination to religious doctrine helps children consolidate the superego and organize a spiritual world view. In addition, institutional affiliation gives children a religious identity and sense of community. As individuals become more self-directed and tolerant of ambiguity, they begin to critically examine their values and beliefs. After a transitional period they relinquish their dependence on religious codes and rely on personal conscience for moral decision-making.

This shift from an external to an internal locus of control does not mean that reliance on inner conscience and commitment to a religious ideology are necessarily incompatible. Many deeply spiritual individuals find meaning and sustenance through a shared set of theological beliefs. Religious observance can either give voice to the convictions of the heart or substitute for critical thinking and personal responsibility. Thus, individuals who compulsively conform to religious codes are distinguished here from people in higher stages who have internalized their religious ideals.

Dogmatic religiosity is rooted in authoritarian parenting. Children of hypercritical and overcontrolling parents develop strong needs for certainty and self-discipline that predispose them to gravitate toward authoritarian religious leaders or groups. Unlike people in stage one, dogmatics received enough consistent love and nurturing to establish a reasonably secure nuclear self. However, affection and affirmation were contingent on the child's absolute complicity with his or her parents' wishes and ideals. Sexual and assertive inclinations, in particular, are anathema to authoritarian parents.

In order to develop an intrinsic sense of self-worth children must be loved unconditionally. Within reasonable limits children should be allowed to express their natural feelings, thoughts and interests. If they are affirmed only when they submit to their parents' aspirations, they become adults who are afraid of their feelings, intolerant of their vulnerabilities and excessively dependent on approval from others. Tormented by guilt and neurotic fears these individuals may turn to authoritarian religion to compensate for their feelings of inadequacy. In addition, their inner "sense of wrongdoing" is congruent with a judgmental religiosity.

Dogmatic faith may also take root in individuals who were overprotected. Some parents try to shelter their children from the harsh realities of life. Many of these parents are well intentioned and have their children's best interests at heart. Nevertheless, by discouraging independent thinking they make it difficult for the child to feel confident and self-assured. Furthermore, children who are not taught to be self-responsible become adults who expect others to make decisions for them. Many feel entitled to an easy life and are easily discouraged and disillusioned when things go wrong.

In addition to stifling the child's initiative, oversolicitous parents unintentionally convey an expectation that the child should not make mistakes or have problems. Children of hypercritical and perfectionistic parents also learn to fear that they will not be loved if they are not perfect.

Some overprotective parents cling to their children out of their own neediness. Insecure parents who depend on their children for appreciation and support place a tremendous burden on them. Sensing that their independence creates pain and anguish for the parent, they feel guilty about their natural thrust toward separation.

Children who feel obliged to conform to their parents' aspirations in order to receive love have difficulty separating from their parents and discovering their own values and ideals. Instead of becoming attuned to their inner voices, they are conditioned to attend to the needs and wishes of others. In addition, they have incorporated the controlling parent into a harsh superego that leads them to be excessively self-critical and perfectionistic.

Individuals reared by domineering parents tend to be particularly wary of revealing any angry or sexually tinged emotions. These neurotic fears are linked to several dynamics. First, because authoritarian parents are conflicted about their own sexual desires, they impose damaging ideas about sexuality onto their children. Second, when children reach puberty, their emerging sexuality and assertiveness remind the insecure parent that their children are becoming independent. These adolescents sense that their individuation is threatening to the parent and feel responsible for their parent's unhappiness.

Finally, adult children of authoritarian families consciously or unconsciously strongly resent their parent's intrusion, intolerance and insatiable demands. Since this underlying resentment conflicts with their needs to please and accommodate their parents, they feel threatened by their angry feelings. In attempting to deny or suppress these negative feelings, they may direct their anger toward themselves and become depressed and self-dissatisfied.

When children are not given opportunities to develop their own talents and interests, but are coerced into molding themselves into replicas of their parents' ideals, they become compliant, unassertive adults who seek validation through approval from others. Their immobilizing fears and diminished capacity for self-assertion are prominent in their religious practice and relationship with God. Having been affirmed for being dependent and self-sacrificing, people in stage two are drawn to religious groups that emphasize self-denial and subordination to religious authority.

Several features distinguish the egocentric and the dogmatic stages. Although dogmatics fear loss of love and labor under an oppressive superego, they do not exhibit the impulsiveness, diffused boundaries, mood swings and abandonment anxiety that characterize egocentric people. In fact, in direct opposition to egocentrics who are *impulsive* and erratic, dogmatics are *compulsive* and constricted. People in stage two strive to earn God's love by repressing their desires and feelings and remaining the acquiescent child.

Unlike the religiously egocentric who suppress their emotions because they are terrified of abandonment and annihilation, dogmatics do not fear retribution or vindictive retaliation. Instead, their excessive need for approval compels them to inhibit any feeling or behavior that they think will result in rejection or criticism. In contrast to egocentrics who strive to *appease* a vengeful God who is easily provoked, dogmatics seek to *please* God in order to earn a privileged place in God's kingdom.

Dogmatics use prayer and confession primarily to quell an inner sense of wrongness or sinfulness. Oriented to associate goodness with compliance, people in stage two feel paralyzing guilt for transgressing the ideals that they uncritically absorbed from their parents. They then project the sadistic superego onto God, whom they experience as critical and displeased. Confession temporarily assuages their guilt.

However, dogmatics cannot experience true forgiveness and reconciliation because they have unconsciously turned God into the disapproving parent who is never satisfied.

Of all religious types dogmatics place the most importance on religious affiliation and participation. For people in stage two a sense of security is attained through identification with a particular faith group. (This also holds true for the spiritual recluse, a sub-type of the stage two category. Even though the spiritual recluse minimizes social interaction, he or she usually maintains a strong identification with a religious tradition.) Since any move toward self-assertion provokes fears of rejection, dogmatics never question or challenge the teachings of their religious community.

In stage two, moral judgment is based on mutual exchange and clearly defined duties and obligations. The individual acts morally in order to appease the demands of conscience and to feel entitled to equal consideration. Primarily grounded in superego anxiety, a morality of reciprocity is provincial and inflexible. However, the emergence of a spirit of justice is a developmental advancement over the heteronomous morality of stage one. A sense of reciprocal obligation distinguishes dogmatics from egocentrics who act morally out of fear of punishment or retaliation. Preoccupation with moral correctness stems from the hope of earning God's love. Confidence in reward for compliance requires internal representations of God that are more trustworthy and less capricious that those that populate the inner world of the psychospiritually egocentric.

In sum, dogmatic faith is focused on institutional allegiance and subordination to religious dogma. People in stage two use "saintliness to serve . . . ego instead of putting . . . ego in the service of saintliness."[4] Their obsession with spiritual perfection points to the extrinsic motivation underlying their spiritual piety.

Psychology's antireligious bias perhaps stems from the preponderance of religiously committed adults who fail to progress beyond the dogmatic stage. Since therapists are in continuous contact with immature adult religious behavior, it is not surprising that they are unattuned to more evolved forms of faith. Nonetheless, a narrow-minded and repressive spiritual orientation does seem to be pervasive among the religiously affiliated.

Individuals in the dogmatic category appear to fall into distinct subgroups. Five types seem prominent: the spiritual legalist, the spiritual martyr, the spiritual crusader, the spiritual intellectual and the spiritual recluse.

THE SPIRITUAL LEGALIST

The Pharisees, who, as depicted in the New Testament, were more concerned with following religious codes than serving God, are prototypical of this sub-group. Beyond simple-minded devotion to parochial beliefs, legalists are punctilious in their religious observance to the point of absurdity. Their scrupulousness and overconscientiousness attest to the degree to which their sense of self-worth derives from being perfect. Insatiable in their need to feel morally correct and certain of God's love, legalists sacrifice independent thinking to the tyranny of religious dogma. In addition, deference to religious injunctions helps them to restrain their sexual and rebellious urges.

Oppressive and rigid families, where behavior is controlled through shame and guilt, are breeding grounds for scrupulosity. Children who are confirmed and admired for proper behavior and berated for self-assertion become emotionally unexpressive, perfectionistic and rigid in their beliefs. They carry their childhood conditioning into their religious life and relentlessly strive to earn God's favor through sanctimonious piety. In addition, they display their self-discipline for others to admire and emulate. Without this admiration they feel devalued and worthless.

Earlier I proposed that mature spiritual devotion balances self-discipline with humble acceptance of God's grace. Proceeding from efforts to appear perfect and morally superior, legalistic "faith" more aptly demonstrates the believers' lack of faith. By relying on their own willpower, discipline and self-control, legalists look to God for approval of their holiness, rather than as a source of spiritual strength. Instead of promoting a spiritual partnership with God, a legalistic orientation encourages compulsive self-reliance.

THE SPIRITUAL MARTYR

Spiritual martyrs impress the naive observer with their selfless concern for the well-being of others. Deeper analysis, however, reveals their selflessness to be the most insidious form of self-righteousness. Recipients of the martyr's magnanimousness are suffocated and manipulated under the guise of love.

Carol Gilligan, author of *In a Different Voice*, a revolutionary treatise on women's moral development, offers a thought-provoking analysis of the feminine ethic of self-sacrifice.[5] Socially conditioned to derive their identity and self-worth through service to others, many women learn to equate goodness with self-denial. Gilligan, however, argues that tying morality to self-sacrifice compromises the individual's integrity and freedom of choice. The ethic of self-sacrifice is a varia-tion of mutual exchange morality in which women submit to consensual judgment about feminine goodness in order to be loved and appreciated. According to Gilligan, a moral crisis may lead one to reflect on the limitations of this position and dissolve the opposition between selfishness and self-care. However, as I have already suggested, moral progression is contingent on a healthy psychological outlook. Women and men who were deprived of adequate nurturing and recognition suffer impairments in their moral and spiritual development.

Spiritual martyrs were compulsive caretakers in their families of origin. Many were in co-dependent relationships with alcoholic parents. In addition to assuming responsibility for the alcoholic's needs, they may have been expected to nurture and support the nonalcoholic parent. Whether or not alcoholism was present, martyrs, as children, were reinforced for their caretaking role in the family. They were affirmed and acknowledged for being super-responsible, patient and self-sacrificing. Their own needs and problems were either ignored or minimized.

Parents may rely on their children to fulfill their emotional needs for many reasons. Spouses in troubled marriages who feel estranged from each other may turn to their children, or a particular child in the family, for comfort and companionship. This was the case with Alice, who is presented in Chapter 12. Single parents in particular may become overdependent on their children for emotional support. Parents who are unable to adequately attend to the child's needs may be overwhelmed because of their own emotional deficits or overextended by externally imposed circumstances such as the death of a spouse, divorce, financial problems, or illness in the family. Children of depressed and distraught parents will assume the caretaking role with the hope that once the parent's needs are met, the parent will then be able to take care of the child.

Compulsive caretakers have learned that their own needs are not as important as those of others. Oriented toward pleasing others and renouncing their own wishes, their religious practice also centers on self-denial and service to others. However, since they unconsciously resent their subservient position, their caregiving has a martyr-like quality that distinguishes injudicious nurturing from mature concern for others.

Religious martyrs are pathologically self-sacrificing for many reasons. Self-denial helps them to feel morally superior and appear generous and noble. Injudicious service to others also stems from the need to feel invulnerable and indestructible. Focusing on the needs of others helps compulsive caregivers deny their own neediness and yearning for nurturing. At the same time, they unconsciously strive to satisfy their suppressed dependency wishes through ostentatious suffering. Religious martyrs hope that if they suffer enough, others will sympathize and rescue them. Finally, the forcefulness and smothering quality of their caregiving suggest that indiscriminate helping serves as an outlet for the repressed hostility that stems from their childhood disappointments. Moreover, when others fail to reciprocate, martyrs can justify feeling angry and abused.

All religious traditions encourage service to others and to God through personal sacrifice. Mature believers of all faiths are distinguished by their selfless love and nonpossessive giving. Their service to others is unconditional and self-replenishing. Spiritual martyrs, on the other hand, use saintliness to meet their own needs for admiration and gratitude. When their caregiving is unacknowledged or unrequited, they become bitter and disillusioned. Compelled to reenact the role of the unselfish and invincible child in their relationships to God and the religious community, spiritual martyrs feel chronically depleted and resentful.

THE SPIRITUAL CRUSADER

The spiritual crusader who "beholds the mote that is in his brother's eye but considers not the beam in his own eye" (Matthew 7:3) epitomizes a more hostile form of dogmatic religiosity. Discomfort with sexual and oppositional urges is managed by focusing on the "sins" of others. Instead of berating themselves for their faults and limitations, crusaders externalize their self-contempt and despise in others the weaknesses that they hate in themselves. To feel scorn at the indiscretions of others is also a means of displacing their resentment toward their captious and intolerant parents.

In contrast to other dogmatic types who tend to be unassertive and emotionally constricted, crusaders are zealous and indignant. Their obsession with annihilating social evil is a defense against acknowledging their own vulnerability to corruption. In addition, condemnation of social immorality enables pugnacious believers to vent their hostility without guilt and to feel morally superior. Preoccupation with the scandalous also allows the more aggressive dogmatic to unconsciously rebel against his self-imposed moral restrictions under the guise of being a respectable and an incorruptible religious servant.

Spiritual crusaders are also determined to convert others to their religious beliefs. Intolerant religious fanatics exhibit an emotional defense that psychoanalysts call "identification with the aggressor." Some children protect themselves against feeling belittled by condescending parents by identifying with them so that they themselves become intolerant and judgmental. Aggressive proselytizing permits crusaders to displace the resentment that they unconsciously harbor toward their domineering parents onto people with religious differences. Fanatics are also intolerant of people with divergent beliefs because ideological differences arouse feelings of doubt that threaten their need for certainty.

Many mature, spiritually committed individuals legitimately oppose violence and immorality and seek reforms through social activism. Crusaders can be distinguished from those who are genuinely dedicated to social ideals by their overzealousness, insensitivity and extreme intolerance.

THE SPIRITUAL INTELLECTUAL

Individuals in this category are intellectually drawn to religious ideas and concepts, but their faith is emotionally impoverished and noncommittal. Habitually immersed in theological or religious studies, spiritual intellectuals are highly introspective and relatively unconcerned with social causes or service to others. They cope with their neurotic fears through intellectualization and emotional detachment.

Superficially, intellectuals resemble legalists in their conscientious pursuit of religious knowledge. However, legalists study diligently to preclude moral error, whereas the intellectually inclined are less concerned with living the law than knowing it. Instead of asserting their moral righteousness, they build self-esteem by exhibiting their intellectual superiority. Undaunted by the inflexibility of conscience that torments other dogmatic types, spiritual intellectuals appear more supercilious and self-assured.

As with other modes of faith, spiritual intellectualism is rooted in childhood experiences. Many authoritarian parents are narcissistically gratified by their children's intellectual accomplishments. Children who happen to be bright may seek affirmation by becoming overachievers. Children who are appreciated primarily for their intellectual capabilities become adults who are compelled to attain academic success in order to feel worthwhile. This compulsive need for intellectual recognition spills over into their religious practice.

With the exception of reclusive types, spiritual intellectuals are the least likely to have strong interpersonal attachments. Their aloofness and dispassion stand in sharp opposition to the compunction of the legalists, the timorousness of the martyrs, and the zealousness of the crusaders. However, their calm exteriors belie their deeply repressed conflicts. Strong conflicting urges to comply with their parents' wishes and to rebel against parental expectations create unbearable tension in the intellectual type.

Individuals in this category are also caught between their longings for emotional closeness and their fears of attachment. They learned that to accept affection is tantamount to thwarting their self-development for the parent's edification. Unwilling to relinquish their individuality, they deny their needs for love and guard their independence. Still, the fact that the concept of God is appealing suggests that their need for attachment to God and others is not entirely suppressed. Their fascination with religious ideas keeps them superficially bonded to a transcendent ideal, while serving to protect them from encountering the anticipated critical and overpowering God. By reading about the religious experiences of others, spiritual intellectuals relate to God vicariously. However, since their feelings are inaccessible, they feel disconnected from others and from God.

THE SPIRITUAL RECLUSE

The spiritual recluse is the most alienated and withdrawn of the dogmatic types. Although most were not cruelly mistreated, they endured relentless criticism and harsh discipline that severely undermined their self-confidence and initiative. Since the slightest rebuff causes them to suffer catastrophic loss of self-esteem, they avoid the intolerable anxiety of associating with people and attempt to fulfill their emotional needs by establishing an exclusive relationship with God. Convents, monasteries, ashrams and religious communes attract reclusive types who seek a safe haven.

There are distinct differences between individuals in this category and spiritually committed people who seek solitude in religious or spiritual retreats. A period of seclusion and quietude helps many to become spiritually rejuvenated and enlightened. Those who occasionally retreat and turn inward return to their former commitments with renewed energy and psychospiritual awareness. Spiritual recluses, on the other hand, permanently withdraw from responsibility and obligation. By restricting their needs to a minimum, the spiritually secluded feel reassured that they will not be hurt or disappointed.

This type is least able to manage sexual or hostile impulses and feels defenseless in social situations. Feeling threatened from within and without, and devoid of affectionate ties to others, these "theopathic" individuals find solace in "an imaginative absorption in the love of God to the exclusion of all other practical human interests."[6] Convinced that their craving for affection will result in humiliation and rejection, they protect themselves from psychic pain and enhance their self-esteem by imagining that they were chosen by God for special consideration. In the process, however, these spiritual types turn God into a shallow child-like figure who is "indifferent to everything but adulation, and full of partiality for his individual favorites."[7]

The spiritually secluded repress their sexual interests by remaining celibate and making God the exclusive object of their devotion. However, the mawkish and naive quality of their devotion indicates that they use religion to create an artificial harmony. Similarly, they submerge all rebellious and oppositional urges. Aggressive feelings constellate around a core of self-contempt that compels some spiritually reclusive people to engage in masochistic ascetic practices or noxious rituals. Self-torturous mortifications or compulsive rituals are also used to atone for mortal weaknesses and to earn a special position in God's kingdom. Moreover, obsessive-compulsive preoccupations serve to distract them from unacceptable thoughts and impulses and their deep yearnings for affection.

Owing to more severe cumulative traumas, this type is the least psychologically integrated and emotionally stable of stage two individuals. Their ability to see God as a constant object and erect a strong repression barrier distinguishes them from self-effacing egocentrics. The spiritual recluse passively wallows in narcissistic piety, instead of actively living in the service of genuine spiritual ideals.

EGOCENTRIC VERSUS DOGMATIC FAITH

Since the egocentric and the dogmatic stages have characteristics in common, further comments are warranted. In particular, as a result of parenting that undermined their initiative and individuality, people in stages one and two are perfectionistic and strive to attain an ideal self. However, despite this resemblance, due to qualitative differences in the parent-child interaction, very specific psychological dynamics differentiate these two types. These are summarized in Table 8.1.

People in stage one were scapegoats for their parents' own rage and disillusionment. Having been repeatedly depreciated and ridiculed, these people feel worthless and self-contemptuous. In stark opposition to the volatile and disorganized households of egocentrics, authoritarian parents are more judicious and predictable. Although they tend to be rigid and uncompromising, overcontrolling parents generally do not make impossible demands or cruelly humiliate their children. Thus, the self-dissatisfaction that plagues people who grew up in authoritarian households is usually attenuated by some degree of self-acceptance.

Because egocentrics were traumatically and persistently belittled or neglected, they feel defeated, demoralized and at the mercy of forces beyond their control. Their brittle facades and grandiose fantasies help sustain a precarious equilibrium that is constantly threatened by a pernicious core of self-hatred. The marked disparity between their actual abilities and their need to be extraordinary prevents them from using their natural talents to form a positive identity. To compensate for their emotional deficits and sense of helplessness, the religiously egocentric seek omnipotence through symbiotic attachment to or magical identification with God or idealized religious leaders.

Table 8.1
Psychological Differences Between Individuals in Stages One and Two

EGOCENTRIC	DOGMATIC
dominated by need gratification, seeks comfort and soothing	seeks reward through conformity and compliance
deficient superego, heteronomous morality	oppressive superego, morality of reciprocity
affective instability, impulsive	emotionally constricted, compulsive
lacks cohesive sense of self, indistinct boundaries between self and others	relatively secure nuclear self
exhibits abrupt shifts in perceptions of others	has achieved full object constancy
attempts to merge with parent-surrogates who are infallibly attuned to their needs and wishes	accepts that others have independent centers of initiative, both fears and desires intimacy
fears object loss, humiliation and retribution	fears disapproval and loss of love

On the other hand, the mixture of harsh discipline with consistent nurturing and contingent reinforcement enables children of authoritarian parents to develop a reasonably intact nuclear self. Their self-dissatisfaction coexists with some inner sense of self-worth. In contradistinction to egocentrics, the dogmatically religious are scrupulous in order to feel self-competent (not omnipotent) and accepted (not symbiotically merged). They learned that affirmation and affection are contingent on proper behavior. As a result, their ideal self constellates around those personal characteristics and aspirations that pleased their parents, and that they assume are pleasing to God. The problem is not that the dogmatic's expectations are too high, but that they are too rigid. When maturational changes or life circumstances steer them toward greater tolerance of themselves and others, they begin the transition to a more mature faith.

NOTES

1. William James, *The Varieties of Religious Experience* (New York: Penguin Books, 1985), 209.

2. Ibid. Quoting Edwin Starbuck, *The Psychology of Religion* (New York: Scribner, 1899), 64.

3. Sigmund Freud, *The Future of an Illusion* (New York: Doubleday, 1927).

4. Fritz Kunkel, *Let's Be Normal* (New York: Ives Washburn, 1929), 278.

5. Carol Gilligan, *In a Different Voice* (Cambridge: Harvard University Press, 1982).

6. James, *Varieties*, 343.

7. Ibid., 346.

Chapter 9

Psychotherapy of the Dogmatic Client

The following lists the features that are common to individuals in stage two.

- overconscientious
- perfectionistic
- compulsive religious activity
- extreme intolerance
- perception of God as judgmental and demanding
- faith attached to religious authority
- conformist identity
- powerful feelings of guilt
- religious fanaticism
- attitude of moral superiority
- afraid of sexual and emotional intimacy
- sin-focused religiosity

RELIGIOUS DIFFERENCES BETWEEN CLIENT AND THERAPIST

Of all spiritual types religious differences between the client and the therapist tend to be most problematic for the dogmatic. However, if handled tactfully and nonjudgmentally, religious differences need not become an insurmountable obstacle to establishing a positive therapeutic relationship. As with other facets of the client's emotional life, his or her feelings about the therapist's faith need to be examined and explored.

It has been my experience that clients with strong religious beliefs inquire about the therapist's religious preference in the initial phases of therapy. An evasive answer may heighten the client's anxiety and lead to premature termination. I have found it most helpful to give a direct response and then explore the client's reactions and concerns.

Usually, the client's initial concern is that the therapist will undermine his or her faith. This fear is particularly salient if the therapist is nonreligious. Because the religious education of some authoritarian religious groups promotes suspicion of psychological methods, dogmatic clients may not be easily reassured that their spiritual concerns will be taken seriously. To complicate matters, their fears of being misunderstood are entangled with their excessive need for certainty and intolerance of differentness.

The therapist should gently probe the client's feelings about their spiritual differences in the same accepting and nondefensive style that undergirds all therapeutic exploration. Helpers who demonstrate tolerance of divergent beliefs challenge the client's assumption that diversity is dangerous and threatening.

Clients should be encouraged to talk about previous experiences where they felt judged or persecuted because of their religious beliefs. Disclosures of encounters with therapists who were perceived to be antagonistic toward the client's religious sensibilities should be taken seriously and thoroughly explored. Secular therapists should not assume that all reports of religious discrimination are the client's projections. On the other hand, religious therapists may take the client's observations at face value and overlook their psychological implications.

After the therapeutic alliance is firmly established, the issue of religious differences usually subsides. However, for others, concerns about the therapist's faith or lack of faith remain in the forefront. Preoccupation with the therapist's spiritual life indicates a strong transference that needs to be processed and eventually interpreted.

CONVERSION EFFORTS

People of different faiths threaten the dogmatic's need for certainty. Individuals in stage two defend against their doubts and uncertainties by attempting to prove the correctness of their spiritual philosophy. Dogmatics who are affiliated with religious groups that encourage proselytizing may attempt to convert the therapist.

Conversion attempts not only reflect a general intolerance of ambiguity, but also may depict reenactments that offer clues to underlying emotional conflicts. Therapists who become drawn into theological debates with evangelizing clients collude with their resistance to deeper self-exploration and miss vital opportunities to promote self-discovery. Instead of countering the client's coercive efforts, the therapist should attempt to understand the unconscious ideas and motives conveyed through religious language. Although each individual will present a unique clinical profile, certain dynamics typify each of the five dogmatic types.

Spiritual crusaders operate from a position that "others are sinful." Their fanaticism, intolerance and disputatiousness are highly antithetical to the therapist's allegiance to humanistic principals. This philosophical difference may strain the practitioner's ability to empathize and create significant tension in the therapy relationship. The hostile countertransference evoked by the fanatical client may be an indication that the therapist has come under the influence of the client's projective identification. Projective identification occurs when the client deposits his or her uncomfortable feelings into the therapist. By identifying with the intolerant and judgmental caretakers, the client unconsciously conveys to the therapist how it feels to be belittled and disaffirmed. The astute therapist will use her own feelings of inadequacy and resentment to empathically understand the client's childhood experience instead of allowing herself to be drawn into a reenactment of that experience.

Through his insistence that others conform to his beliefs, the dogmatic crusader unconsciously communicates his frustration with parents who undermined his individuality. The therapist who fails to understand this central dynamic may be diverted from the therapeutic task by the client's theological bantering and become locked in a transference-countertransference struggle that recapitulates the sadomasochistic quality of the parent-child interactions.

The spiritual legalist is an obsessive-compulsive type who sees others as "less righteous," rather than more sinful. This difference in interpersonal orientation is more than semantical and indicates an important distinction in the use of defense mechanisms. The crusader is externally focused and uses projection. He identifies with the critical parents and expects others to be perfect. In contrast, the legalist is internally focused and has introjected the voice of the critical parents. He expects himself to be flawless and morally impeccable in conformance with his parents' wish for a perfect child. Since religious differences awaken an intolerable sense of uncertainty, the legalist proselytizes primarily to defend against doubt. He is less concerned with the therapist's salvation than with convincing himself of the correctness of his religious beliefs and spiritual values.

In addition, the legalist is highly dependent on approval from others. Those who belong to religious groups that seek new converts and emphasize "witnessing" may attempt to earn the accolades of their faith community by persuading the therapist to join.

Conditioned to be caretakers at expense to themselves, spiritual martyrs may feel responsible for the therapist's spiritual life. However, because their concern for others commingles with strong feelings of resentment and needs to be appreciated and affirmed, conversion efforts are tinged with self-pity. Their position that "others are ungrateful" serves to distract them from their vulnerability and neediness. Therapists who reject their proselytizing efforts without exploring their deeper motives collude in supporting their masochistic style.

Spiritual intellectuals are less interested in convincing the therapist to adopt their faith than in impressing her with their knowledge of religion. Their position that "others are unenlightened" helps them to avoid intimate relationships and feel superior. They may be quite knowledgeable about different religions, yet they fail to creatively assimilate divergent beliefs into a self-affirming personal faith.

Believing that "others are spiritually inferior" helps spiritual recluses mask an inner sense of inadequacy and unworthiness. These individuals are most interested in cultivating an exclusive relationship with God and least likely to impose their spiritual philosophy on the therapist.

Dogmatic clients are most resistant to psychological interpretation of spiritual issues. Therefore, the therapist must convey a genuine appreciation of the healthy aspects of their spiritual orientation. She must take time to become knowledgeable about the client's faith. This effort not only strengthens the therapeutic bond, but also helps the practitioner distinguish the distortions in the client's religious ideology from its healthier components.

After the therapist feels confident that she has some understanding of the client's psychospiritual functioning, her task is to help the client become curious about his inner world. The therapist might arouse curiosity by wondering why it is so important to the client that they hold similar beliefs. With patience and skillful probing this inquiry will usually lead to fruitful self-discovery.

ANGER AND SEXUALITY

Authoritarian parents are particularly threatened by their children's sexuality and assertiveness. Those who use religion to support their own neurotic fears induce similar fears in their children. Dramatic and exaggerated warnings from parents and religious educators about the dangers of lustful and aggressive feelings compromise the child's development of healthy emotional expression.

Distortions of religious imperatives to "turn the other cheek" produce obsequious individuals who allow others to take advantage of them. Religious therapists should remind dogmatics that such imperatives were warnings against revengeful retaliation and were not meant to discourage normal assertion of legitimate rights or appropriate expression of disappointment.

Since dogmatics were rewarded for compliance, they are likely to be overaccommodating in the therapeutic relationship. Helping them to acknowledge their irritation over a cancelled or rescheduled appointment or over an inaccurate interpretation can be a first step in promoting more assertive behavior. In addition, the therapist can help the deferential client to recognize the irrational fears that accompany his nonassertiveness. For example, the overcompliant client may dread the therapist's disapproval, believe that his treatment will be terminated if he does not placate the therapist or anticipate that the therapist will not tolerate an opposing opinion. The spiritual martyr may resent a cancellation or schedule change, but feel that it is selfish to consider his own needs and desires. By exploring these feelings with an accepting therapist, the client not only gains permission to be more assertive, but also begins to uncover the childhood roots of these neurotic fears. He associates his complicity with memories of being indoctrinated with the virtues of self-denial or criticized for asserting his individuality.

Dogmatics value emotional calmness not only because they are conditioned to be even-tempered, but also because unconsciously they harbor deep resentment over their parents' failure to nurture their emerging selfhood. The fact that compliance with the parents' ambitions is often supported through religious doctrine makes the unconscious wish to defy the parents' authority even more threatening to the client with strong religious sensibilities. However, because dogmatics are not consumed by the seething rage that characterizes those in stage one and because their anger is not associated with the egocentric's fear of retaliation or abandonment, their anger phobia will gradually diminish through a permissive and accepting therapeutic milieu.

Sexuality constitutes another problematic area for dogmatically religious clients. Damaging messages about sex from parents and religious educators become internal saboteurs of the individual's sexual enjoyment. It is not reasonable to suppose that an individual can repress every sexual thought, fantasy and feeling until the wedding night and then suddenly become a passionate sexual partner.

The dogmatically religious experience a great deal of guilt and embarrassment over sexual issues. Therefore, therapists should not probe too deeply into the clients' sexual fantasies or activities until a strong therapeutic bond has been established. Before exploring the childhood roots of their sexual concerns, therapists may need to reeducate these clients and normalize their sexual feelings. In particular, therapists may have to dispel myths about masturbation, oral sex, orgasm and sexual fantasy. My experience with dogmatics, especially those from fundamentalist Christian backgrounds, is that they confuse feelings with actions. They erroneously conclude that having sexual feelings for or fantasies about someone other than their spouse is equivalent to committing adultery.

Some dogmatics are uncomfortable with all sexual feelings and even feel guilty about marital sex. These clients may unconsciously be fearful of being a sexual adult due to anxiety about separating from their parents. Guilt about relinquishing the parents for the love partner may underlie the dogmatic's fear of sexual and emotional intimacy. Pervasive and chronic sexual anxiety or inhibitions may also stem from strong, unresolved Oedipal conflicts.

Poor self-esteem may also interfere with sexual pleasure. People who feel bad about themselves have difficulty believing that others find them sexually desirable. Since feelings of inadequacy are pervasive among people from authoritarian religious backgrounds, it is not surprising that many fail to develop a positive sexual identity.

Dogmatic clients may find it excruciating to talk about their personal thoughts and feelings, especially those that make them feel most vulnerable. They assume that the therapist will criticize them as harshly as their parents have done in the past. Therefore, unconditional acceptance is crucial to maintaining a therapeutic alliance with these clients. Although most therapists strive to be uncritical, secular therapists may unintentionally convey a judgmental attitude toward clients with strong religious beliefs. In particular, they must guard against equating sexual value differences with sexual inhibition. The decision to wait until marriage before engaging in sexual intercourse is not necessarily indicative of sexual repression. Satisfying sex in marriage depends on healthy sexual attitudes, not the number of premarital sexual experiences. If, after his emotional conflicts have been reasonably worked through, a client makes a conscious choice to defer sexual gratification for religious reasons, the therapist must respect this decision and resist the temptation to liberalize the client.

Resolution of emotional conflicts should help dogmatic clients become more spontaneous. As an adjunct to the analytic work, relaxation or meditation techniques and assertiveness training can help these clients become less emotionally constricted. *Beyond the Relaxation Response* by Herbert Benson, which incorporates the "faith factor" into a method of achieving a state of deep relaxation, and *The Assertive Christian* by Michael Emmons and Rev. David Richardson are two resources that are particularly suitable for working with religious clients.

GUILT AND SELF-FORGIVENESS

Dogmatics are tormented by neurotic guilt. Parental scoldings for the child's imperfections become introjected and masquerade as true conscience. As adults they are drawn to authoritarian religious groups because an oppressive religiosity resonates with their basic sense of inadequacy. The dogmatic's bond to a critical God recreates the childhood experience of never being good enough.

Children of authoritarian parents live in constant fear of losing their parents' love if they fail to measure up. To alleviate their anxiety these children try to be perfect. Those with strong religious sensibilities eventually transfer these dynamics into their relationship with God. As a result, they become obsessive about conforming to the details of their religious doctrine. Religious therapists who urge a more self-forgiving attitude without first modifying the dogmatic's harsh superego are unlikely to produce more than superficial changes in the client's spiritual practices.

Secular therapists, on the other hand, may wish to cleanse the client's spiritual thinking of ideas about sin, repentance and atonement. However, feelings of accountability to God and participation in rituals for expiation are not in themselves unhealthy or indicative of deeper emotional conflicts. Secular therapists should respect those religious conduits through which the client attains a sense of forgiveness for moral violations. These spiritual practices should be challenged only when they are masochistic and self-punishing or when they consistently fail to ameliorate feelings of guilt. Persistent inability to feel exonerated through prayer, confession or purification rituals suggests that the client's early parent-child interactions were excessively guilt-producing.

In addition to neurotic guilt that is rooted in the oppressive superego, the dogmatic suffers from existential guilt. Existential guilt is a vague sense of uneasiness that occurs when we suppress our individuality and fail to achieve our potential. Unlike neurotic guilt, which is irrational and repressive, existential guilt awakens suppressed needs and mobilizes growth. It is the thrust of the inner self striving for expression.

People in stage two have so thoroughly identified themselves with the role cast for them by their parents that they are cut off from their inner needs and desires. In the process of molding themselves into model children, they diminish themselves. We have already discussed how the dogmatic's sexual self may be compromised.

Unconsciously, or perhaps consciously, the dogmatic knows that he is not functioning at full capacity. He feels that self-discontentment that occurs when an individual's inner thrust toward individuation and self-actualization is thwarted. Feelings of existential guilt and anxiety are distress signals from the healthy core of the personality.

In order to grow beyond their paralyzing guilt, dogmatics must first confront the fact that their ideals and ambitions are not their own or God's, but were imposed on them by their parents. Until they disentangle their own inner convictions from the parental introjects, they will feel divided and torn. The client may have so thoroughly assimilated the messages of his overbearing parents that it may take months or even years before he allows his true feelings to surface. With patience and skillful probing he will eventually recognize that his guilt is his way of exonerating his parents for their unreasonable demands.

The client's experience of being accepted and understood by a nonjudgmental therapist helps him to be more patient and gentle with himself. As he is liberated from the compulsion to comply with his parents' wishes and expectations, his greater self-tolerance is mirrored in his relationship with God. Relieved from the burden of feeling responsible for his parents' happiness, he stops thinking of God as rebuking and criticizing him. The locus of his faith shifts to a more compassionate and nurturing deity. Following this inner transformation, it is likely that he will relinquish his former religious ties and seek a more tolerant religious community. My work with Patty, the focus of Chapter 13, illustrates this process in greater detail.

SEPARATION AND PERSONAL RESPONSIBILITY

Overreliance on dogma stunts development of personal responsibility. Although their conscientiousness in carrying out their duties and obligations makes people in stage one appear to be super-responsible, closer analysis of their moral reasoning (Chapter 8) indicates that they suspend the critical thinking that is necessary for developmentally advanced decision-making.

The therapist's task is to help the client move from an external to an internal locus of control. Nonjudgmental exploration and the permissive therapeutic milieu help the client penetrate the repression barrier to discover his true values and ambitions. At first, this self-discovery feels exhilarating and liberating as neurotic compulsions loosen their stranglehold. However, after the initial excitement, the compunction for abandoning the parents' most cherished ideals may puncture the dogmatic's delight in his emerging self-determination.

Perhaps, as was true of Alice, who is presented in Chapter 12, the dogmatic on the verge of transition is most afraid of becoming permanently estranged from his family if he makes decisions that are antithetical to family traditions. This fear of being repudiated is the original unconscious force that leads the dogmatic to cling to the illusion that his family's religious ideals are his own.

When the client's fears of separation and individuation are derepressed and become conscious, they can be rationally examined and challenged. Despite the fact that authoritarian parents usually voice strong opposition and searing disapproval over their children's choices, they rarely disown their children for deviating from family traditions.

As clients become less reliant on approval from others, they are less willing to sacrifice their individuality for their parents' approbation. However, clients should be prepared for the fact that an assertion of independence will initially upset the family homeostasis. Concurrently, they can be encouraged to relinquish responsibility for the reactions of others.

The work of separation cannot begin until the client acknowledges and works through his anger and resentment so that he no longer needs to feel guilty as a means of exculpating his parents. My clinical work with Alice and Patty illustrates how healing the rageful inner child enabled them to accept their parents' limitations without justifying or rationalizing their behaviors. While more than willing to forgive their parents' failures, they refuse to be intimidated by their intolerance. These women have relinquished the role of the acquiescent child and insist on relating to their parents as an adult. After a painful period of readjustment they learned that separation does not mean disconnection.

As clients begin the process of separation, they enter the transitional phase of psychospiritual development. At this stage clients replace servile fear with personal and moral responsibility.

Chapter 10

Stage 3: Transitional Faith

During the normal course of development major transitions, which parallel other developmental changes, occur in the spiritual lives of most adolescents and young adults. Significant among these changes are advancements in moral reasoning. Healthy adolescents progress from an ethic of reciprocity to a morality of "mutual interpersonal relations."[1] Although the intellectual development of adolescents contributes to their more sophisticated moral reasoning, intelligence alone is insufficient for mature moral decision-making. In addition to cognitive growth, a healthy psychological outlook is necessary for moral and spiritual development.

As a result of significant inner conflict, individuals in stages one and two remain impoverished in their moral judgment. Egocentrics act morally in order to avoid punishment, and dogmatics act fairly in order to receive equal treatment. Dogmatics with masochistic tendencies feel morally compelled to deny their own needs in the service of others or God. However, compulsive self-denial is damaging to oneself and others. People who are co-dependent not only deplete themselves, but also enable others to be irresponsible and abusive. Moreover, compulsive caretakers do not sacrifice out of mature concern for others, but because they have a tremendous stake in maintaining ideal images of themselves as loving and compassionate. Unconsciously, martyrs suffer in order to feel morally superior.

A morality of interpersonal mutuality is under the dominion of a healthier superego. People who experience an intrinsic sense of self-worth have a greater sensitivity to the needs of others. They act morally because they appreciate that others are entitled to the same rights and privileges as themselves. Unlike those in earlier stages who consider the needs of others out of self-interest, individuals in stage three can imaginatively walk in another's shoes and experience true compassion and mature concern.

Notwithstanding that people in the transitional phase of spiritual development have a more evolved standard of ethics than those in earlier stages, their moral decisions are still strongly influenced by the opinions of others. "In stage three actions are right if they conform to the expectations of one's 'significant others.' A powerful motive of stage three moral action is to please those persons who matter greatly and not to disappoint their opinions and expectations of us."[2] However, their desires to please are motivated more by their affectionate feelings for significant others than by fears of abandonment or loss of love.

As individuals in stage three struggle to forge a personal identity and unifying philosophy of life, they become more rebellious and self-determined. Yet despite the common belief that adolescents typically reject their parents' ideals, studies suggest that most teenage rebellion centers on styles of dress and musical tastes. Adolescents typically retain their families' core values.

Their thrust toward more independent decision-making, combined with their strong need to stay connected to significant others, can lead transitionals to feel divided and torn. For example, parents and religious educators usually encourage adolescents to remain sexually abstinent. At the same time, teenagers' biological urges and peer pressure tempt them to become sexually active. Conflicting loyalties and ambivalent feelings may lead individuals at this stage to oscillate between celibacy and sexual indulgence. As the adolescent becomes less dependent on the opinions of others and gains the maturity to manage strong conflicting feelings, he or she will adopt a style of sexual conduct that is congruent with his or her self-chosen spiritual values.

At stage three the approval of family and friends enhances the individual's sense of solidarity, but is less crucial for regulating self-esteem. People at this level can risk disapproval without experiencing a dramatic loss of self-worth. Furthermore, because they are more emotionally integrated and self-accepting, they do not feel overwhelmed by their sexual and adventurous desires. Finding constructive outlets for their emotions and learning appropriate restraint are major developmental tasks for individuals in psychospiritual transition.

A more positive outlook also helps transitionals feel less threatened by their spiritual doubts and uncertainties. Their eagerness to critically examine their spiritual beliefs and values and to forsake outmoded concepts and ideals is the hallmark of transitional faith.

Many religiously committed people believe that doubt is synonymous with lacking faith. Just the opposite is true. Mature faith is fashioned from storms of doubt. Skepticism and uncertainty are paths to higher levels of psychospiritual integration. A recent study of age and religious orientation suggests that a period of spiritual searching bridges the individual's evolution from an extrinsic religiousness to a healthier intrinsic commitment.[3] According to the study, this transition seems to peak during adolescence.

Although the impulse toward a faith that is more inclusive and tolerant usually emerges in adolescence, many people cling to their childhood beliefs. Individuals who are deeply entrenched in self-defeating styles are unlikely to progress psychospiritually without professional help. However, whatever the circumstances that lead to critical reflection on previously held values, people at this stage experience a spiritual identity crisis.

When individuals begin to challenge the validity of their most sacred beliefs and ideals, significant inner tension and emotional disequilibrium are unavoidable. Those who enjoyed an unquestioning relationship to God and to their religious community may experience a profound sense of loss. These feelings of grief and groundlessness are usually temporary and subside within a reasonable period of time.

Transitionals may try on different ideologies before selecting and consolidating a personally meaningful spiritual philosophy. Their curiosity may prompt them to switch religious affiliations or investigate nontraditional faiths. Others may denounce their former allegiances and become apostates. Research indicates that while many disaffiliates eventually choose a faith, others remain religiously unaffiliated.[4]

In sum, an inner thrust toward separation and independence leads individuals in stage three to critically reflect on their spiritual beliefs and values. As they become disembedded from the world view that they previously took for granted, they may feel anxious and confused. Support and encouragement will help them to forge a spiritual path that is congruent with their emerging ideals.

NOTES

1. See Chapter 10 in James Fowler, *Stages of Faith: The Psychology of Human Development and the Quest for Meaning* (San Francisco: Harper & Row, 1981).

2. Ibid., 74.

3. P.J. Watson, Robin Howard, Ralph Hood and Ronald Morris, "Age and Religious Orientation," *Review of Religious Research* 29 (1988): 271-280.

4. C. Kirk Hadaway, "Identifying American Apostates: A Cluster Analysis," *Journal for the Scientific Study of Religion* 28 (1989): 201-215.

Chapter 11

Psychotherapy of the Transitional Client

Clients in stage three can be expected to exhibit at least some of the following characteristics of transitional faith:

- Religious questioning and doubt
- Critical examination of religious beliefs and commitments
- Exploration of divergent faiths
- Affiliational switching
- Spiritual identity confusion
- Reassessment of ideals leading to inconsistent application of moral values
- Transition from an external to an internal locus of authority

SPIRITUAL IDENTITY CRISIS

The transitional client's evolution toward a more sophisticated spiritual apperception is both liberating and anxiety-provoking. If the client has or had a strong attachment to a religious community, the surging doubts and uncertainties of the transitional stage may lead to a spiritual identity crisis.

In addition to the analytical work, the transitional client needs a great deal of support in order to endure the sense of groundlessness that occurs as former beliefs are critically examined. The therapist can reassure the client that few sincerely spiritual individuals have lived their faith without confronting some anguish along the way. Clients in stage three might be encouraged to read historical accounts of spiritual leaders who encountered storms of doubt. The story of Job, which illustrates how spiritual regeneration can eventually be cultivated out of despair, may help calm the spiritually frazzled.

Owing to a dramatic shift in their cognitive and psychological functioning, transitional clients are expected to be emotionally erratic. The astute therapist learns to distinguish spiritual languor from clinical depression. As clients become more responsible for their moral choices and acquire a greater sensitivity to others, they often suffer an existential angst that may resemble a mood disorder to the naive observer. However, normal psychospiritual troughs are balanced by a capacity to experience positive feelings. Persistent feelings of emptiness or hopelessness that do not remit within a reasonable period of time indicate that the client is experiencing significant inner tension beyond that associated with normal developmental changes.

Transitional clients who were deeply entrenched in highly authoritarian religious traditions may be particularly susceptible to feelings of depression and anxiety. Therapists who fail to appreciate the unique vulnerabilities of these clients may misinterpret their emotional lability as a sign of regression and feel that their therapeutic efforts were unsuccessful.

Clients who challenge venerated ideals usually discover that family and friends are unsympathetic toward their revitalized spiritual interests. If the client renounces her former faith, she will experience a sense of loss that is directly proportional to her degree of attachment to the religious community. If the religious community was also the center of the client's social life, she may feel tremendously lonely and sad.

In their eagerness to celebrate the client's renunciation of an oppressive religiosity, therapists may fail to appreciate the client's grief. However, clients who do not mourn the loss of people and ideals that were highly significant in their lives carry residues of hurt and disappointment that may impede further spiritual development.

Former members of highly authoritarian religious groups associate traditional religion with oppression and therefore may either disaffiliate or become involved with nontraditional faiths. Furthermore, the client's negative attitude toward religious institutions may extend to the religious therapist, especially if the therapist shared the client's former faith. The negative transference will be intensified if the therapist feels disappointed or anxious about the client's unorthodox beliefs. Religious therapists who fail to manage their own countertransference toward apostate clients convince them that freedom of choice is dangerous and leads to abandonment.

Assuming the religious therapist has successfully resolved his own countertransference, he may still be unconsciously drawn into a projective identification. A client's relentless disparagement of the therapist's faith can cause even the most tolerant and patient therapist to become defensive. By identifying with the aggressor, the client deposits her own rejected self into the therapist. Instead of being drawn into the reenactment, the therapist must help the client redirect her anger toward those who have belittled her spiritual quest. Eventually, she will mourn the loss of her former religious ties and develop a more self-affirming spiritual identity.

EXAMINING THE SPIRITUAL QUEST

A period of spiritual searching characterizes the transitional phase of development. The client's spiritual quest may steer her toward faiths outside the Judeo-Christian tradition. Investigation of divergent ideologies is both an expression of rebellion against former beliefs and a genuine search for ideals that are more congruent with inner convictions.

Even though therapists must not assume that unorthodox spiritual interests reflect emotional conflict, a client's angry repudiation of her former faith should be explored. When spiritual issues are at the forefront of the therapeutic enterprise, therapists should probe a client's motives for pursuing a particular faith. Two brief clinical examples will underscore the importance of thoroughly examining the psychological implications of a radical shift in religious orientation.

Becky, a former Baptist, was intent on converting to the Islamic faith. Her primary reason for selecting Islam was that except for prohibitions against marrying outside the Moslem tradition, she "could find nothing wrong with it." Yet she was willing to either remain single or find a Moslem spouse so as not to violate the one Islamic belief that she found offensive.

Becky's father was a Baptist minister. In contradistinction to the Christian fundamentalist belief in the wife's submission to the husband's authority, Becky's mother ruled the household. Her father tolerated his

wife's mood swings and angry outbursts with passive resignation. By
being the perfect child, a feat accomplished through strict obedience to
religious prescriptions, Becky assuaged her mother's harsh disposition.
Her strong religious allegiance was facilitated by her attachment to her
father, who was patient and loving toward Becky. However, Becky's
bond with her father was tainted with rage at his complicity in her
mother's abuse.

Throughout the duration of our work Becky clung tenaciously to an
idealized image of her family. Her refusal to acknowledge her rageful
feelings toward her parents contributed to strong unconscious wishes for
retaliation. She retaliated by repudiating the family's religious identity
and selecting a faith that is antithetical to the Baptist tradition. Thus,
her renunciation of her former faith did not constitute a spiritual
progression, but was instead an act of hostility. She merely substituted
one religious doctrine for another. Her orientation toward religion
remained dogmatic and inflexible. Both her previous allegiance to the
Baptist faith and her conversion to Islam served extrinsic motives.

Cindy, a practicing Catholic, was also intrigued by Islamic spirituality. She was introduced to Moslem doctrine through a course in
religious philosophy and was impressed by points of convergence
between the Christian and the Islamic traditions.

During Cindy's early adolescence her parents divorced due to her
father's increasing abuse of alcohol. Shortly after the divorce her father
remarried, causing Cindy to feel replaced and abandoned. Later she
discovered that he had been unfaithful to her mother during the latter
years of their marriage. Her efforts to convince him to seek treatment
were met with angry retorts and further withdrawal. Fearful of losing
him completely, Cindy suppressed her outrage at his betrayal and
desertion by viewing him as a victim of his alcoholism. Directing her
anger toward his "disease" enabled Cindy to retain the image of the
ideal father of her early childhood.

As her illusion about her father's recovery began to erode, Cindy
experienced a crisis in her faith. No longer dissuaded by her rational-
izations, her rage surfaced with full force, leading her to project the
conflict with her father onto her relationship with God. She became
convinced that because she could no longer tolerate her father's
womanizing and drunkenness, she was a "bad" daughter. She was
equally convinced that God would not forgive her impatience and
intolerance. Cindy's spiritual crisis represented an unconscious
projection of her own inability to forgive her father for being a "bad"

therapist

father. My acceptance and validation of her anger toward her father enabled Cindy to work through her feelings of disappointment and disillusionment. She was eventually able to relinquish her hope for resurrecting the father she had known before his alcohol addiction.

As therapy progressed, Cindy learned to distinguish forgiveness from exoneration. She subsequently forgave her father for his failures and inadequacies, but at the same time she holds him accountable for his actions. She feels tremendous sadness at witnessing his mental and physical deterioration, but no longer holds herself responsible for his recovery.

Paradoxically, Cindy's relinquishing of the "ideal" father did not diminish, but rather strengthened, her attachment to him. Even though his own spiritual life faltered, she treasures memories of attending church with her father. Her affiliation with the Catholic community has been enriched, rather than depreciated, by her progress in therapy. Having attained a more integrated and reality-based image of her father, she no longer feels compelled to project her negative feelings into her relationship with God. Cindy's openness and curiosity about other religious philosophies indicates that her reattachment to the Catholic church is not just a revival of infantile wishes.

Unlike Becky, Cindy wished not to renounce her Christian heritage, but to expand her spiritual understanding by incorporating beliefs from other traditions. However, Cindy's maturity is indicated not by the fact that she retained her former faith, but by the greater degree of conscious control that she exercises in her choices.

FEAR OF COMMITMENT

Successful resolution of the transitional stage leads the individual toward a flexible and personally integrating spiritual commitment. Although a period of spiritual floundering is expected to precede the reconstruction phase, endless questing without making at least a tentative choice leaves the individual adrift in a sea of meaningless relativism. Without firm spiritual guidelines the inquiring, but uncommitted, often oscillate between opposing values and life styles.

The transitional client who fails to adopt a consistent spiritual philosophy within a reasonable period of time is usually afraid of commitment. Intense fear of commitment that permeates many facets of the client's life is indicative of an underlying personality disturbance that requires in-depth exploration. However, if the client's indecisiveness is specific to her spiritual life, rather than being a pervasive characterological style, the therapist may be more directive in his approach.

Clients who were affiliated with authoritarian religious groups learned to associate spiritual devotion with loss of autonomy and individual choice. Former members of rigidly fundamentalistic congregations will be legitimately distrustful of any organized spiritual setting. Therapists who have established a network of sensitive and trustworthy religious professionals can steer those clients who wish to retain their religious heritage toward innovative and progressive congregations within their particular faith traditions. I often refer clients to religious professionals who are unperturbed by the uncertainty and doubt that are concomitant with the struggle toward mature faith. Most secular therapists must rely on trusted clergypersons to correct the theological distortions that may be contributing to the client's noncommittal attitude. Clients who wish to remain open-minded skeptics can become involved in eclectic traditions that encourage free-thinking and personal spiritual growth. The Quaker, Unitarian, Unity and Bahai faiths welcome members with divergent religious backgrounds and spiritual beliefs.

Adult children of interfaith marriages may also have difficulty choosing a faith. In their book *Between Two Worlds*, journalists Leslie Goodman-Malamuth and Robin Margolis address the issues faced by grown descendents of Jewish-Christian marriages. Even though the book is targeted for readers of mixed Jewish-Gentile heritage, the authors' insights are applicable to others who are struggling to reconcile a dual religious identity. Therapists working with clients from dual-faith families will find this book to be a valuable resource.

While many find the diversity and stimulation of religiously eclectic homes spiritually nourishing and enriching, other religious hybrids feel confused and torn by their dual allegiances. Whether raised in one parent's faith, in both faiths, in a third "compromise" religion or with no religious affiliation, adult children of intermarriage are highly sensitive to conflicting messages transmitted by their parents and members of their extended family. In addition, people of dual religious heritage are often scorned by religious communities and society in general.

Transitional clients from dual-faith homes may be reluctant to select a faith for fear of causing one parent to feel rejected. If religious differences were a source of tension in the home, the client may be spiritually immobilized by conflicting loyalties. Therapists must help these clients disentangle their own spiritual needs from their parents' spoken and unspoken wishes.

If they feel compelled to follow the faith that was selected for them, clients may feel shameful about their interest in the religious persuasion of the "out-parent." The client's sense of guilt will be exacerbated if she belongs to a religious group that is contemptuous toward her other half. If she copes with these fears by suppressing or hiding her curiosity about her other heritage, she will feel divided and disconnected. Clients who complain of feeling hypocritical about their religious observance and estranged from their faith communities may be reacting to suppressed desires to explore other faiths. Similar dynamics may also occur in clients from single-faith homes who wish to investigate other traditions.

Some people of dual religious heritage choose to maintain connections with both worlds. Those that select a primary religious identity continue to feel some allegiance and attachment to their other half. Therapists can normalize the client's desire to integrate her religious loyalties and encourage her to find a congregation that will welcome her mixed heritage. If a client was exposed to vehemently opposed religious cultures, she will need to tolerate unresolvable differences and accept the fact that total reconciliation of beliefs is impossible.

In order to maximize our ability to assist clients who are struggling to establish spiritual identities, therapists of all religious faiths, as well as the religiously unaffiliated, must be familiar with the core beliefs of the traditions that compose our religiously pluralistic society. If encouraged to explore their options, most transitional clients will find a faith community that is reasonably compatible with their spiritual needs.

PSYCHOSPIRITUAL GROUP THERAPY

Rationale

Many transitional clients benefit from group treatment, either as the sole type of treatment or in combination with individual therapy. A religiously diverse, spiritually focused therapy group, if skillfully facilitated, can be a positive force in promoting the psychospiritual development of its participants. Individuals in spiritual transition who continually receive reprisals for their unorthodox beliefs may find reprieve through group alliances that support their curiosity and individuality. In addition, clients may feel less compelled to project a saintly facade in a spiritually mixed environment.

Interreligious settings provide vital opportunities for learning about unfamiliar faiths and spiritual philosophies. Group participants of divergent spiritual orientations can help each other replace damaging religious beliefs with more positive affirmations. As members interact, they are likely to become more comfortable with religious differences and relinquish stereotypical thinking about people of other traditions.

Philosophy

The nonsectarian emphasis distinguishes the group modality presented here from therapy groups offered in religious settings.[1] In contrast to theologically anchored groups that assume allegiance to specific core beliefs, the spiritually eclectic context encourages a norm of open inquiry that supports each individual's quest to discover his or her own spiritual truth and meaning.

Although spiritual in focus, the experience is firmly grounded in the principles and techniques of traditional group therapy. I draw heavily on such standard texts as Irvin Yalom's *The Theory and Practice of Group Psychotherapy* and *The Theory and Practice of Group Counseling* by Gerald Corey. Therapists who conduct spiritually focused therapy groups should have extensive knowledge of group dynamics and skill in group facilitation.

Consistent with the theoretical underpinnings of this book, a primary goal of the psychospiritual therapy group is to assist members in understanding how their spiritual dilemmas may relate to deeper emotional issues. A cohesive and trusting group provides a unique forum for the intensive self-exploration that precedes spiritual transformation.

Group Composition

A spiritually focused therapy group can be the ideal treatment for clients with religious and spiritual concerns. Nevertheless, therapists must conduct a thorough assessment to determine whether or not a particular client can benefit from group work. As with other theme centered therapy groups, this approach will not be the treatment of choice for all clients with religious issues. Groups offered in religious settings should be considered for clients who feel threatened by a spiritually diverse milieu. Others are better served through individual treatment alone.

Contraindications for group therapy in general are applicable to psychospiritual groups. Exclusion criteria include acute psychotic or mood disorders; strongly narcissistic, antisocial, paranoid, schizoid or borderline traits; dread of self-disclosure; alcohol or drug dependence; low motivation for change; low psychological-mindedness and high somatization. In addition, clients who are likely to be unnecessarily provocative or assume a deviant role are not suitable for group therapy. Individuals in acute distress, who would otherwise be appropriate for group treatment, should wait until the immediate crisis has subsided before entering group treatment.

Because of their emotional lability, vulnerability to severe regressions and orientation to need gratification, group therapy is not recommended for egocentric clients. Individuals in stage one are better served through intensive, long-term individual therapy. As mentioned previously, some may require inpatient treatment and psycho-pharmacological management.

Group therapy is also contraindicated for the fervent, proselytizing dogmatic client, who is likely to see the group as an opportunity for "witnessing." Fundamentalistic individuals of nonproselytizing faiths may use the group to display their piety. In either case, the condescending attitudes of dogmatics who are deeply entrenched in elitist religious groups are not conducive to promoting a supportive therapeutic atmosphere. However, entry into a group can be the optimal intervention for the stage two individual on the brink of spiritual disenchantment.

Clients in stages three and four are usually the most receptive to joining a therapy group. Since their curiosity and motivation for change are at a peak, a group setting can produce a synergistic effect that maximizes their potential for psychospiritual growth.

The ideal group is heterogeneous with respect to gender and religious background and composed of from six to ten members. Although I screen rigorously for psychological fitness, I do not exercise any exclusionary criteria in terms of spiritual beliefs.

Group Structure and Process

Psychospiritual groups can be time-limited or time-unlimited, depending on therapeutic goals or logistical constraints. To accommodate the changing schedules of college students I conduct ten to fifteen session groups that coincide with the fall and the spring semesters. However, groups of limited duration do not allow for in-depth examination of childhood issues. Upon termination of the group, some students opt for individual treatment to delve more intensively into issues that surfaced in the group.

A group meeting schedule of one- to two-hour sessions once a week is typical for outpatient work. I use an unstructured format to allow members to address the issues that concern them.

The first session begins with introductions and discussion of confidentiality, attendance and ground rules. After these preliminaries members and leaders share their goals and expectations for the group experience. Participants are reminded that the group is therapy and not a "rap" session. With the ending of the first meeting, members are given written guidelines to orient them to group work. Experts in group psychotherapy often recommend that therapists devote adequate time to preparing participants for group involvement.

If skillfully facilitated, the group will evolve through several levels of interaction. Therapists who are unfamiliar with the stages of group development are urged to consult the literature on group dynamics. Even though the group's process is fairly predictable, its content may feel strangely unfamiliar to therapists who conduct traditional therapy groups in secular settings. Issues that are likely to emerge in a spiritually focused group include (but are not limited to) feelings of guilt or anxiety about defecting from the family faith, apprehension about religious doubts and uncertainties, inner conflicts with frightening God images, problems of interfaith relationships, feelings of meaninglessness or spiritual apathy and spiritual perfectionism.

In sum, therapy groups with a spiritual theme offer participants an opportunity to recapitulate and work through negative religious influences, explore alternative faiths and consolidate a spiritual identity without theological constraints. A safe, nurturing atmosphere that encourages self-exploration, constructive confrontation and mutual support holds special potential for assisting individuals in developing a more evolved spiritual capacity.

Alice, who is presented in the next chapter, began her therapeutic journey by participating in a psychospiritual therapy group that I conducted. After the group ended, she continued with me in individual therapy to further explore troubling issues that had emerged in the group. Alice's conflicts and concerns are typical of people in the transitional phase of psychospiritual development.

NOTE

1. Development of this group model is elaborated in two previous articles. See Vicky Genia, "Interreligious Encounter Group: A Psychospiritual Experience for Faith Development," *Counseling and Values* 35 (1990): 39-51; and Vicky Genia, "Psychospiritual Group Counseling for College Students," *Journal for College Student Development* 31 (1990): 279-280. Despite the use of different names for this treatment modality, its purpose and goals are consistent throughout my writings. Because "exploration" connotes a discussion group, "encounter" conjures up images of the ill-reputed gestalt-type groups of the 70s and "interreligious" may seem to exclude the religiously unaffiliated, I finally settled on the term *psychospiritual therapy group.*

Chapter 12

The Case of Alice: God of Ideals

Alice is an attractive, energetic twenty-five-year-old graduate student. Her vivaciousness and personable style make her romantically desirable and popular among her peers. She freely admits that she thrives on the attention and yearns for affectionate attachments. Yet her fear of intimacy compels her to keep a comfortable distance from others. This ambivalence is also mirrored in her spiritual quest. Although she speaks positively about her Jewish heritage, she is drawn toward religious traditions that are highly antithetical to the Jewish faith. Moreover, she fails to experience real intimacy with God or a religious community despite her deep longing to feel spiritually connected.

When Alice consulted me, she was overwhelmed with mixed emotions that followed a brief and intense romantic encounter with a "born again" Christian. Her involvement with this man precipitated a spiritual crisis, which prompted her to seek therapy. Initially, she kept personal disclosures to a minimum and, knowing about my interest in religious issues, used our sessions to ponder philosophical questions and ideas. As therapy progressed, however, Alice realized that unresolved emotional conflicts contributed to her spiritual concerns and inability to

Reprinted, with changes, from *Counseling and Values* 37 (1992) pp. 15-24. Copyright © 1992 ACA. Reprinted with permission. No further reproduction authorized without written permission of the American Counseling Association.

establish sustaining ties to a faith community. She was convinced that she had failed to live up to God's ideals and that God was disappointed in her.

Alice is the middle of three daughters from an upper-middle-class Jewish home. Her father is thoroughly devoted to being a successful entrepreneur and leaves the domestic and caretaking responsibilities to his wife. Even though he is not deeply religious, Alice's father expects his daughters to find suitable Jewish husbands and to remain sexually abstinent until marriage. Despite his conservative values, he had an affair with one of his clients. Alice's parents considered divorce, but decided to reconcile after the affair was terminated. Except for his sexual indiscretion, Alice has only fond memories of her father and feels much closer to him than to her mother.

In contrast to her father, Alice's mother flaunts her religious devoutness and seems to derive significant gratification from her role as the suffering servant. From Alice's descriptions, her mother appears to give not out of selfless concern for others, but to feel avenged through her moral superiority. Her mother's smothering caregiving also seems to be a desperate plea for attention and affection. She hopes that if she gives enough, she will receive love and appreciation in return.

Alice admits that she feels restricted by her mother's suffocating presence. She deeply resents her mother's philosophy of duty and self-sacrifice and her extreme religious intolerance. However, the fact that her mother is more intensely involved with Alice than with the other family members leads Alice to feel responsible for her mother's happiness.

Alice's own faith is colored by her conflict between her desire for affectionate relationships and her fear of intimacy. Her wish to bond with a divine Other and belong to a spiritual community is overshadowed by her tremendous fear of being smothered and disillusioned. She finds a compromise solution by remaining the open-minded skeptic in search of truth. Alice's brief involvements with divergent religious traditions provide her with some outlet for her spiritual strivings. However, because she feels disconnected and distant from God, her explorations leave her feeling empty and spiritually unfulfilled. The fact that she experiments with different faiths through brief romantic encounters with religious men suggests that her spiritual and interpersonal difficulties are intricately related. As we examined these relationships in therapy, the connections between her emotional and her religious conflicts were brought to light.

In the early phases of her courtship with John, Alice was most impressed with his firm commitment to conservative religious values. She envied his confidence about his convictions, which contrasted with her wavering and doubt. Yet she vehemently resisted his efforts to convert her to a fundamentalist Christian faith. The certitude and unquestioning devotion that she first admired quickly began to feel controlling and intrusive.

At the time Alice was only partly aware of the emotional forces that were impinging on her. She had become quite attached to John and was fearful of losing him if she did not accept his faith. At the same time, her resentment of his conversion efforts drove a wedge between them. That John was less than sympathetic toward her misgivings about his beliefs also contributed to the mounting tension between them. These dynamics directly parallel Alice's relationship with her mother. In order to stay connected to her mother Alice feels that she must embrace ideals that stifle her independence. The deterioration of her relationship with John served to further convince her that to accept affection she must discard her autonomy.

Alice's conflicts with her father were also reenacted in her relationship with John. Like her father, John believed premarital sex to be prohibited. At first, Alice felt reassured by his convictions because it protected her from the temptation to act on her sexual desires. Still, her disillusionment following her father's affair seriously impaired her ability to trust men. Subconsciously, Alice wondered if John would betray her as her father had betrayed her mother.

It is difficult for Alice to acknowledge her resentment toward her father. To preserve the idealized attachment to her father she projects her anger onto the men that she dates. Thus, she expects that they will have negative reactions to her sexual feelings toward them. Since Alice was anxious about revealing her sexually tinged feelings, she was cautious and reserved in her expressions of affection toward John. Interpreting Alice's aloofness as disinterest, John abruptly ended the relationship.

By depositing her anger toward her hypocritical father into her romantic relationships, Alice unconsciously reenacts the rupture in her bond with her father. This repetition serves to deflect her rage and disappointment at her father's betrayal. It also prevents her from establishing healthy and satisfying intergender attachments.

Not surprisingly, Alice's conflicts with her parents are also mirrored in her feelings about God. Her God is a condescending, intolerant deity who demands self-denial and sexual purity. These are the ideals that were instilled in her by her parents. God has been assimilated into the role of the harsh superego that ensures her unquestioning compliance with family values. By feeling guilty for her sexual desires she avoids her outrage at her father's adulterous behavior. Believing that she has disappointed God is preferable to admitting her disappointment in her father.

Having learned from her mother that love requires unending self-sacrifice, every failed relationship serves to further reinforce Alice's belief that self-assertion and independent thinking lead to rejection and loss. Frightened of ending up alone, Alice has periods where she devotes her energy to accommodating and pleasing others. Assuming that God, too, has no patience with her doubts and uncertainties, Alice seeks a faith that she can wholeheartedly embrace. Still, she refuses to surrender her autonomy. Rather, her efforts to please others and God coexist with a resistance to losing her individuality, leading her to alternate between conforming to and rebelling against values imposed upon her. This struggle to follow her inner convictions distinguishes her from people in earlier stages and indicates a transitional stage of development.

Issues of identity and intimacy typify early adult development, but for Alice they are complicated by disruptive emotional experiences. Her disillusionment over her father's affair constitutes a major obstacle to forming a healthy sexual identity and genuine loving relationships. In addition, other more subtle conflicts with her mother are also linked to her interpersonal problems and painful struggle for independence.

Alice remembers having very little interaction with her mother during early childhood. This awareness came as a surprise to her since she remembers being close to her mother during her high school years. While her father was involved with another woman, her mother turned to Alice for comfort and support. At that time Alice's older sister was planning to marry, and her younger sister only added to her mother's burdens. Feeling lonely and depressed, her mother depended on Alice for affection and nurturing. Since the problems in her parents' marriage remain unresolved, her mother continues to rely on Alice for her emotional needs, thereby discouraging Alice's separation and independence. Dissatisfied with herself and her marriage, Alice's mother is unable to help her daughter through the difficult process of discovering and consolidating her own unique identity. That her mother responds to Alice's infatuations with unnecessarily blunt comments about promiscuous women serves to further undermine Alice's sexual development.

Prior to her father's affair Alice's younger sister consumed most of her mother's time and energy, causing Alice to feel disregarded and abandoned. This earlier emotional loss intensifies Alice's desire to retain the closeness that she experienced with her mother during high school. As a result, she is especially fearful of disappointing her mother and provoking her disapproval. At the same time, her efforts to conform to ideals that stifle her natural spontaneity and curiosity make her feel trapped and lifeless. Alice's relationship to John served to heighten her defiance against her mother's ethics of submission and self-denial, reintroduced to her in the form of Protestant fundamentalism. When she sought therapy, she could no longer fit comfortably into the mold that was cast for her. Alice turned to me as a surrogate parent who would not be disappointed by her attempts to make independent choices.

Coinciding with tremendous needs to formulate her own values and control her destiny, Alice feels an obligation to live up to her parents' ideals. While partly rooted in unconscious fears of losing their love, this sense of responsibility also represents a genuine loyalty to parents who provided much that was positive and loving in spite of their failures and shortcomings.

Conflicting wishes to retain her parents' ideals and to renounce these standards account for Alice's failure to establish a consistent value system. Alice desperately wishes to be close with her parents, and especially her mother, without feeling inextricably bound to their rigid morals. Not able to please her parents and herself at the same time, Alice oscillates between a celibate and a sexually active life style. Her inability to develop a personally meaningful faith also relates to this dynamic. Unwilling to adopt her mother's oppressive brand of religion or her father's puritanical standards and fearful of espousing a self-chosen faith that is incongruent with her parents' values and beliefs, Alice avoids religious commitment.

Alice's simultaneous attraction and opposition to her parents' ideals was a key dynamic in her affair with a deeply religious Moslem. Alice was initially attracted to Mohammad because of his espoused moral values and dedication to work. Unconsciously, she was drawn to those qualities that she admires in her father. However, she was in deep conflict over their sexual intimacies. On the one hand, Alice enjoyed the attention and the physical pleasure. Her sexual expression was also an assertion of independence and separation from her parents' rigid standards. Her wish to please Mohammad and her fear of losing his affection also contributed to her willingness to have sex with him. On the other hand, Alice felt guilty for violating her parents' morals and was fearful of displeasing and disappointing them. Her guilt was a defensive maneuver that kept her from acknowledging her disappointment in them, especially her father. Her unconscious wish to punish her father is manifested in her romantic involvements with non-Jewish men. The intensity of her anger toward her hypocritical father and her authoritarian mother is indicated by her involvements with faiths so antithetical to the Jewish tradition.

As her relationship with Mohammad deepened, he became extremely jealous and repeatedly accused Alice of flirting with other men. Later she discovered that he was involved with another woman. His double standard was painfully reminiscent of her father's behavior and caused feelings of outrage. Alice eventually understood that her reluctance to acknowledge her anger toward her father leads her to reenact her disappointment with men who reject or betray her. Since these men purport to be deeply religious, each rejection leads her to feel more disinclined to make a religious commitment.

Yet despite her disenchantment and religious floundering Alice retains a passion for truth that fuels a healthy spiritual striving. An authentic desire for a spiritual commitment enables her to wrestle with her ambivalent feelings and endure the tremendous discomfort of confronting her religious doubts and questions. Even though her attachment to God is tinctured with negative emotions, Alice possesses a core of basic trust that contributes to an inner conviction of a transcendent goodness that she has yet to discover. This optimistic outlook, coupled with her open-mindedness, keeps her from becoming bitter or cynical. As Alice confronts her resentments and fears and becomes more confident in herself, she will be able to make a religious commitment that is harmonious with her emerging ideals, values and life choices.

Chapter 13

Stage 4: Reconstructed Faith

Under favorable conditions the exploration, critical reflection and introspection of the transitional stage will culminate in commitment to a self-chosen faith that is congruent with one's ideals and inner conscience. At this stage an intrinsic spiritual commitment promotes a sense of purpose and life meaning. Religious doctrine, when important to the individual, is interpreted more flexibly, and moral reasoning is guided by a higher level of superego development.

Unfortunately, "superego" is equated with sadistic infringements of guilt and anxiety, the self-accusations that torment us whenever we indulge in forbidden thoughts or wishes. However, in healthy personalities the ego ideal claims a more distinct piece of the superego. In contradistinction to the shame-provoking voice of the introjected critical parent, the ego ideal represents the inner loving parent. Since maturity is a striving toward positive ideals, instead of away from feelings of wrongdoing, the primacy of the ego ideal is a more evolved moral adaptation.

This distinction can be clarified by looking at the married individual who is tempted to have an affair. Spiritually committed people in the egocentric, dogmatic and reconstructed stages who oppose extramarital sex may decide against the affair. However, in each stage the moral decision-making process will be very different. Persons in stage one will forgo the affair out of fear of being caught and abandoned by their spouses or punished by God for committing adultery. The dogmatically religious will remain faithful to avoid feeling guilty and to prove their moral impeccability. Moreover, if they expect their spouses to be faithful, dogmatics feel compelled to honor the marriage contract as well. Individuals in stage four, on the other hand, will resist temptation by focusing on the positive ideals of commitment and responsibility. The decision to refuse the illicit encounter is motivated by love and respect for their spouses. The intrinsically committed do not act morally out of fear or obligation, but because they feel a sustained responsibility for the welfare of others.

At stage four, moral behavior is governed by social contract. At this level "guiding moral values and principles . . . have validity and applicability apart from the authority of the groups or people holding them and apart from the individual's own identification with these groups."[1] Guided by a mature superego, people in the reconstructed phase of development adhere to religious codes because they are felt to be in harmony with their inner convictions.

People at this level feel a sense of connection to an affirming world. Their faith is grounded in the disposition to trust and the inner sense of well-being that are the psychological inheritance of those who were adequately nurtured and affirmed in childhood. God is felt to be an ally and source of sustenance. The prayers of those who pray include thanksgiving, praise and devotion. Unlike those in earlier stages, people in stage four accept their human limitations without apology or shame. Confession, if practiced, relates to realistic feelings of accountability. After feeling remorseful for wrongdoing, the intrinsically religious accept God's forgiveness and then make restitution whenever possible.

Research conducted in the area of intrinsic-extrinsic religiousness indicates that, overall, individuals with an intrinsic faith commitment tend to be more psychologically and emotionally healthy than those with self-serving religious motivations.[2] The psychospiritual reconstruction that follows the transitional phase helps them to establish a firm, but flexible, commitment to chosen ideals. Invigorated by an increasing reliance on personal conscience, individuals in stage four relinquish outmoded beliefs and select an ideological perspective that fits a reshaped identity.

Nevertheless, people in the reconstructed stage have not cultivated the tolerance for ambiguity and uncertainty or the ability to appreciate the paradoxical and multifaceted nature of spirituality that characterizes those in stage five. Although extricated from the tyrannies of dogma and external authority, stage four faith retains residuals of the absoluteness and elitism that characterize dogmatic religiosity. Notwithstanding their tolerance of divergent beliefs, these individuals are disinclined to worship with people of different faiths. If their ideological consolidation becomes impermeable to new spiritual insights, their faith will not undergo further progressive transformations. Experiences that expand and enrich the spiritual outlooks of the intrinsically religious may promote their spiritual evolution by enabling them to become more open to "the voices of one's 'deeper self' " and more receptive to a "more dialectical and multileveled approach to life truth."[3]

Before I met Patty, she had never questioned her religious convictions. She was unperturbed by spiritual matters until her intolerable rage toward her father surfaced in the therapy. As she relinquished her idealized attachment to her father, she experienced a painful loss of faith. In confronting her feelings and challenging her former beliefs, Patty was able to reconstruct and reconsolidate her former faith.

THE CASE OF PATTY: GOD OF LOVE

Patty is a thirty-two-year-old, single, Catholic woman. She is somewhat quiet and reserved, but can be conversational and friendly in social situations where she feels comfortable. Her desire to become more confident and assertive initially prompted her to seek therapy.

Patty is the oldest of four children from a working-class family. Her father is a simple man with strong traditional values and tremendous pride. He is conscientious and hardworking, but rigid in his beliefs and intolerant of divergent opinions. His self-righteousness and extreme intolerance are compounded by a volatile temper that occasionally erupts into violent outbursts. As a result, he inspires fear in family members, rather than genuine respect.

Patty's mother is a kind, but extremely passive, woman who is overshadowed by her husband's domineering presence in the family. Attempts to assert her own needs are met with resistance and retaliation. To preserve family peace she assumes a subservient role and complies with her husband's wishes and demands.

In order to earn her father's affection and appreciation Patty became the model child. Through her academic excellence, proper social behavior and compliance she secured her father's love. Yet even though she enjoyed her status as the favored child, she also sensed the tenuousness of her position, which was contingent upon maintaining excellence and obedience. Patty defended against full awareness of the conditional nature of her father's love by identifying with the ideal self that her father affirmed. However, because of this strong identification, she was intolerant of her imperfections and vulnerable to feelings of failure.

Patty's need to please her father in order to feel worthwhile generalized to her religious life so that her relationship to God and the church was characterized by conformance to ritual and dogma. The Catholic emphasis on God the Father and the paternal priesthood contributed to the ease with which Patty transferred her feelings toward her father onto God and the church. Her communication with God consisted of recitations of formal prayers such as the Our Father, Hail Mary and the Apostles' Creed. Patty rarely talked with God about her inner feelings and needs in a conversational manner.

This formality was also present in her dialogues with her father. Fearful of displeasing him, Patty was careful not to express opinions or concerns that would upset him. Her pseudo-maturity made it easy for Patty's father to confide his problems and concerns to her. While her position as confidant exposed Patty to her father's vulnerable side, thereby stirring strong compassion for him, she also resented the burden of being the idealized daughter. Furthermore, she experienced tremendous guilt for replacing her mother, whom Patty believed should be the person to nurture and comfort him.

As a child and an adolescent Patty felt comfortable in the Catholic church, which in many respects was similar to her family. The church's subordination of women and emphasis on obedience and good works were congruent with her upbringing. Moreover, Catholic reverence for the self-sacrificing, quiet suffering of Mary, the mother of God, appeared to Patty to normalize her father's authority and rationalize his unreasonable behavior.

Patty was predisposed to extract from her faith the features that resonated with her personal experience and to ignore those elements that contradicted that experience. Therefore, she was attuned to the dogmatic and oppressive elements of the Catholic community and unacquainted with the nurturing and inspiring spirituality of more liberal and progressive congregations.

As Patty became exposed to different philosophical world views in college, she experienced an uncomfortable state of dissonance that motivated her to examine the values that she had previously uncritically accepted. Her exposure to feminist philosophy, in particular, caused her to challenge the appropriateness of some of her father's attitudes and behaviors. In addition, through new friends and acquaintances she witnessed life styles that stood in radical opposition to her own rigid upbringing. Prior to college Patty had rarely interacted with her peers outside of school and church. Her social encapsulation insulated her from experiences that might have led her to question the normality and appropriateness of her father's restrictions and control.

The dissonance between her old values and an emerging liberal outlook caused Patty to become anxious and depressed. Her family environment was not conducive to nurturing the seeds of personal change that were developing from the social and intellectual stimulation of college life. In order to avoid confrontation with her father, Patty pretended to be the acquiescent child, while her inner sense of herself was becoming radically transformed. Her father, also wishing to retain the idealized daughter, pretended not to notice that Patty was becoming more independent and assertive. Patty felt as if she walked a tightrope. If she deviated too far, she risked losing her father's love and respect, not to mention financial support for her education. Yet, by continuing to be submissive and overaccommodating she sacrificed her integrity and emerging autonomy.

This conflict finally culminated in an emotional and spiritual crisis after Patty completed her graduate training. Perceiving that her evolving identity was a constant threat to her favored position with her father, Patty became increasingly depressed and withdrawn. She was especially frightened by her capacity to be more assertive because it aroused the rage that she felt toward her father. She repressed her anger by retreating to her former compliant personality style. Unfortunately, her reticence and unassertiveness were impediments to her professional and social development. This may have been less problematic for her if not for her father's expectations that Patty be socially and financially successful. This expectation placed Patty in a terrible bind. The personal skills that she needed to be successful in order to please her father were also traits that displeased him.

At the same time that she was becoming more distant in her professional and social interactions, Patty began to withdraw from her religious involvement. She attended mass less and less frequently. She was unable to recite her familiar prayers or receive the sacraments and became profoundly disturbed by her "lack of faith." As we explored these events, the dynamics underlying her spiritual crisis unfolded.

Patty's transference of feelings toward her father onto God and the church was facilitated by the paternal elitism of traditional Catholicism. Unconsciously, she felt that God would also disapprove of her inner growth and critical examination of her ideals, including her religious values. As with her father, Patty experienced God's love as conditional upon obedience and submission to His will. Yet, unlike with her father, she could not pretend compliance to an omnipotent God whom she felt already judged and condemned her. Patty was unable to derive comfort from the nurturing, feminine aspects of the Catholic faith because she associated femininity with weakness, masochism and inadequacy, the qualities that she despised in her mother and in herself.

A critical point in the treatment occurred when Patty related a dream in which she confronted the devil. She understood that the devil was a personification of unacknowledged parts of herself. Fearful of disapproving others, especially her father, Patty despised the qualities in herself that contradicted her ideal self. She was especially contemptuous of the angry feelings that were buried deep inside and projected this "evil" part of herself onto the devil figure in the dream. Specifically, Patty was infuriated by her father's sadistic treatment of and rigid control over the family. Furthermore, she was outraged at her mother's failure to intervene effectively against her father's harsh discipline and unreasonable demands.

Several factors contributed to Patty's ability to confront and work through her anger toward her parents. First, and most important, was a foundation of basic trust grounded in a satisfying symbiotic phase and reinforced during childhood development. Patty's mother, despite her limitations, was consistent and affirming in her love and affection for her children. In addition, Patty's position of favor with her father attenuated the effects of his harsh discipline by enabling her to experience and integrate his gentle and affectionate side as well. These positive parental qualities formed the cornerstone of her spiritual development and transformation of her faith.

The path to discovering a loving God was not an easy one for Patty. Fortunately, her basic orientation of trust enabled her to use the therapy relationship to shed the crust of her false self. Within the therapeutic ambience of acceptance and empathic understanding, Patty allowed the rageful inner child to emerge and heal. It was only after she acknowledged the repressed anger that she could begin to forgive her parents for their failures. Released from the need to idealize them in order to shelter herself from her rage, Patty could see her parents as products of their own dysfunctional families and inadequate parenting. By accepting her anger as a legitimate and intricate part of herself she became more emotionally spontaneous and appropriately assertive in her interactions with others. Most important, Patty became more tolerant of herself and relinquished her compulsion to be perfect. This enabled her to accept God's forgiveness and unconditional love.

One day, toward the end of treatment, Patty spontaneously entered a church as she was walking home. As she sat quietly before the altar, she was infused with a sense of "God as Love." In that moment her faith was rekindled as she experienced God's gentleness and compassion. Following this spiritual awakening Patty returned to the Catholic community. Although she still challenges some of the teachings of the church, her commitment to the positive elements of the Catholic faith undergirds her personal spiritual growth and devotion to God. Patty's involvement with groups seeking reforms within the church gives her a sense of belonging to the religious community despite her liberal beliefs. Her participation also provides her with opportunities for sharing her faith through social action.

NOTES

1. James Fowler, *Stages of Faith: The Psychology of Human Development and the Quest for Meaning* (San Francisco: Harper & Row, 1981), 83.

2. For reviews of this research, see C. Daniel Batson and W. Larry Ventis, *The Religious Experience: A Social-Psychological Perspective* (New York: Oxford University Press, 1982); and Michael Donahue, "Intrinsic and Extrinsic Religiousness: Review and Meta-Analysis," *Journal of Personality and Social Psychology* 48 (1985): 400-419.

3. Fowler, *Stages of Faith*, 183, 198.

Chapter 14

Stage 5: Transcendent Faith

Transcendent faith is the highest level of spiritual development. The endpoint of maturation is an ideal that even the most spiritually enlightened can only approximate. Even though it is impossible to attain spiritual perfection in this life, the hallmark of mature faith is an enthusiasm for wholesome living. Like Saint Paul, the spiritually mature aspire to saintliness, while humbly accepting their limitations and shortcomings in their daily spiritual walks (Philippians 3:13, 14).

The following discussion highlights some of the qualities that characterize those in stage five. This presentation is offered with humble awareness that no psychological analysis can adequately explain their extraordinary compassion and conviction. Passionately attuned to universal ideals and a transcendent actuality, individuals at the apex of spiritual development are visionaries who inspire people of all faiths.

Keep in mind that these criteria are not intended to be absolute standards or to represent the ideals of any particular faith. Rather, this chapter posits some identifying characteristics of mature faith, to be expanded, refined or modified in light of further reflection or examination.

1. *Transcendent relationship to something greater than oneself is the cornerstone of mature faith.* According to William James, "the sense of Presence of a higher and friendly Power seems to be the fundamental feature in the spiritual life."[1] Mature faith, however, is more than intellectual acknowledgment of an ultimate reality. It requires a

response to this reality that leads to a constructive transformation of our lives.

How the human self meets the Divine is a subject of considerable speculation and controversy. Whereas traditional believers discover the essential Other through religious teachings, the nontraditional seeker looks for God within the self. Perhaps the most unorthodox among the spiritually inquiring, humanists prefer to purge the spiritual dimension of the supernatural and search for the transcendent in the outer limits of human consciousness.

Erich Fromm's depiction of the individual's encounter with the All epitomizes the humanistic perspective on transcendent experience.[2] According to Fromm, we all have a psychospiritual need for an object of devotion. When feelings of reverence are aimed toward a higher power, we feel spiritually connected and whole. However, Fromm believed that this higher power is found within the self and that God is but "a symbol of *man's own powers*." A meeting of the Divine occurs by "breaking through the confines of one's . . . ego and . . . getting in touch with the excluded and disassociated part of oneself, the unconscious."[3] Thus, faith in God is simply faith in life and in ourselves.

It is important to note that Fromm disagreed with Sigmund Freud's conception of the unconscious as a reservoir of seething destructive impulses. In Fromm's analysis, the unconscious contains both the highest and the lowest, the unscrupulous and the philanthropic urges. Since our forbidden wishes coexist with a profound capacity for love, they need not be feared or repressed. By opening the door of the unconscious and getting in touch with both the self-serving and the humanitarian sides of ourselves, a creative integration transpires in which human passions are tempered by conscious control and commitment to universal ideals. This expansion of consciousness and realization of human potentialities is, according to Fromm, the essence of religious experience.

It is not surprising to find threads of the James tradition in Fromm's religious theorizing. Most impressed by the diversity of religious experience, James was convinced that the spiritual impulse is not initiated by an external power, but rather derives from the "higher faculties of our own hidden mind."[4] He believed that this outer region of human nature "is conterminous and continuous with a MORE of the same quality, which is operative in the universe outside of him, and which he can keep in working touch with."[5] Inspired by the spiritual forces that flow through the door of the unconscious, individuals create

or choose a religious ideology that is compatible with their tempera-
ments and intellectual capabilities. Despite his determination to discard
theological "overbeliefs" and explain the religious impulse as a natural
phenomenon, James left open the possibility of a divine existence on the
"farther side of the MORE."

Carl Jung, a prominent contemporary and contender of Freud, also
located the transcendent in the outer region of human consciousness.
He depicted God as an "archetype" that is revealed to the individual
through the "collective unconscious."[6]

The deepest layer of the psyche in the Jungian schema, the collective
unconscious, retains primordial images of experiences that have been
part of our species' repertoire since its evolution. Jung referred to
these psychological motifs as archetypes. For example, all human
infants are nurtured by an adult caretaker. Therefore, there exists in
the collective unconscious a mother archetype that predisposes infants
to become instinctively attached to their mothers. Because some form
of religious worship has occurred throughout history and across
cultures, spiritual symbols and God images are also embedded in the
psyche of every individual. Religious seekers meet the Divine through
the God archetype, which is the psychological heritage of the
commonwealth of being.

For Jung the religious pilgrimage is to bring into consciousness the
fundamental wisdom that has been preserved in the collective
unconscious. Whereas Freud adamantly believed that religion is
detrimental to human growth and development, Jung was equally
convinced that the religious quest is a journey toward the highest
potentials of humankind. Thus, in contrast to his rival, Jung viewed
spirituality not as a regressive phenomenon, but as a progression toward
greater wholeness.

Two additional points will serve to qualify Jung's sympathetic
attitude toward religion. First, his psychotheology exalts the individual
and excludes the community aspects of faith. The sacred is found
within the self. Jung was biased toward faiths that insist on the
essential identity of God and man, and he expressed antipathy toward
traditions that externalize the deity. Like James, Jung believed that
allegiance to a religious creed prevents us from encountering our inner
spiritual consciousness and therefore contributes to a shallow and
narrow-minded faith state.

Second, although Jung maintained that spiritual enlightenment is
available to everyone through the collective unconscious, he was careful

not to comment on the theological authenticity of the God archetype. Since Jung believed that the collective unconscious preserves those experiences that promote human survival and progression, he was convinced that its religious images were positive forces in the psychic economy. Whether or not this universal spiritual consciousness originated from divine inspiration had no bearing on its psychological value and therefore was not of concern to him.

In the humanistic tradition represented by Fromm, James and Jung, the sacred resides in the higher nature of individuals and may be accessed by opening the door to the unconscious. Even though neither James nor Jung vigorously denied the possibility of a supernatural deity, their analysis of religious experience assumes the essential identity of person and God. The experience of being seized by a power outside of ourselves is due, they claim, to the tremendous affective intensity and temporary disorientation that occur when material that was previously unconscious suddenly invades one's field of consciousness. Loathe to concur with supernatural explanations of religious phenomena, humanists place supreme confidence in the natural spiritual potential of human beings.

Buddha also excluded a supernatural God from his spiritual teachings. Buddhism is unique among the major religions in that it proposes a path to self-transcendence, or Nirvana, without theological presuppositions. Followers of Buddha denounce all formal dogmas and anthropomorphic metaphors and resemble humanists in their search for spiritual wholeness through inner personal enlightenment. Unlike secular humanists, however, Buddhists do not strive for spiritual completion by expanding the self to incorporate a higher consciousness. Instead, they seek to dissolve the boundary of the finite self by extinguishing ordinary consciousness and human desire. Notwithstanding that humanism and Buddhism are highly divergent philosophies, both concur that the Divine is nothing but the apex of self-evolution.

Some religiously committed individuals find the notion that the self can attain godhood preposterous, if not heretical. Included among the religious traditions that emphasize the essential otherness of God are Christianity, Judaism, Islam and dualistic (*bhakti*) Hinduism. The idea that God is simply a higher state of self is anathema to affiliates of those faiths that underscore the separateness of the Creator and the creatures of creation. The thoughts of a *bhakti* Hindu aptly and concisely summarize this position.

He who worships God must stand distinct from Him. . . . Mother and child are
two, if not, where were love? . . . Where were joy, if the two were one?
Pray, then, no more for utter oneness with God.[7]

Pantheistic thinkers and certain Hindu and Christian mystics tread a
middle ground between dualistic traditions and those that make no distinction between the human and the divine. They underscore the *unity*,
but not the *identity*, of God and the individual. In nondual Hinduism,
for example, the supreme reality is diffused throughout the universe and
yet is present in each individual. The spiritual goal of the mystical
Hindu is to unite his personhood with Brahma, the Beyond, which
penetrates all living things. Through mastery of the *raja* or the *jnana*
yoga, the devotee attains a state of *Samadhi*, or merger with God.
Similarly, pantheism emphasizes absorption of the self into the All.

This brief summary highlights the multitude of possibilities for
understanding the human-God encounter. The varieties of religious and
spiritual experiences are virtually unlimited. Regardless of how
individuals apprehend their interactions with God, mature faith is
reflected in the ways in which their responses to the transcendent transform their lives.

2. *Life style, including moral behavior, is consistent with spiritual
values.* Mature faith involves a conscious effort to harmonize our lives
with our spiritual values. This effort requires sensitivity to prevailing
community standards and honest self-examination. Neither unquestioning submission to religious authority nor sporadic allegiance to ideals
that tantalize the intellect constitutes a healthy spiritual commitment.

For the spiritually mature, religious or spiritual beliefs provide a
unifying philosophical underpinning that guides their moral decisions
and integrates their life experiences. The ideals and ethics of people in
the transcendent stage are highly concordant with their life styles and
inner convictions.

3. *Commitment without absolute certainty is essential for spiritual
health.* Gordon Allport's contention that "mature religious sentiment
is ordinarily fashioned in the workshop of doubt"[8] reflects the paradox
that spiritual convictions are strengthened by critically examining them.

The demand for absoluteness impedes psychospiritual growth in
several ways. First, religious certainty is an illusion that requires a
great deal of repression and denial to sustain. Complete spiritual

understanding eludes us all. Historical accounts of spiritual leaders in all traditions attest to the fact that even the most enlightened encounter storms of doubt. Indeed, faith with certainty is a contradiction in terms. It is not necessary to accept on faith that which is unquestionably established as true.

Second, the illusion of certitude contributes to an attitude of self-righteousness and moral superiority that diminishes our spiritual vision and leads to interpersonal problems. Third, a legalistically based sense of moral correctness leads the believer to relinquish responsibility for the consequences of his or her actions. Moreover, overreliance on fixed rules of ethics strains the ability to untangle conflicting obligations. Conversely, the courage to tolerate ambiguity and explore all reasonable alternatives is likely to produce creative solutions to moral dilemmas.

Finally, those that numb themselves to all shreds of doubt are most susceptible to a crisis of faith because their spiritual foundation rests on a precarious "all or none" philosophy. If tragic or fortuitous circumstances disrupt this tenuous equilibrium, they may lose faith entirely and enter a spiritual vacuum.

Although some religious groups accuse the doubtful of being faithless, faith and doubt are not mutually exclusive. Commitment to a spiritual ideology can be held tentatively *and* vigorously. Everyday we make important decisions without complete information or knowledge. For example, medical illnesses are treated with available methods until more effective treatments are discovered and refined. Similarly, our faith can guide us even as we seek greater truth and understanding.

Openness to revision and responsible commitment complement, rather than oppose, one another. While tentativeness minimizes fanaticism and religiocentricity, commitment generates discipline and consistency. Furthermore, a firm commitment is a good prophylactic against existential despair or cynicism. Gandhi eloquently described his gift for feeling conviction in the face of uncertainty.

I worship God as Truth only. I have not yet found Him, but I am seeking after Him. . . . But as long as I have not realized this Absolute Truth, so long must I hold by the relative truth as I have conceived it. That relative truth must, meanwhile, be my beacon, my shield and buckler.[9]

Doubt cannot coexist with arrogance. Therefore, healthy skepticism fosters an attitude of humbleness. Our willingness to be vulnerable and hold our faith open to correction helps us to sustain a steadfast, but flexible, spiritual outlook that is likely to endure tests of faith.

4. *The spiritually mature appreciate spiritual diversity.* This criterion of mature faith follows logically from the previous one. Fromm reminds us that "no man can presume to have any knowledge of God which permits him to criticize or condemn his fellow man or to claim that his own idea of God is the right one."[10]

Individuals in stage five do not simply tolerate religious diversity, while insulating themselves from divergent beliefs and claiming certitude for their own formulations about God. Those at the pinnacle of spiritual development expand their visions of truth by critically examining and creatively assimilating ideas from people of all persuasions.

I recently conducted a psychospiritual group at a university counseling center. The group was intended for students with religious and spiritual concerns. The purpose of the group was to help participants grow spiritually by affording them the opportunity to share their concerns in a spiritually diverse therapeutic context.

One of the students who participated in this group, a young Jewish woman, expressed reservations about formulating a personal religion by weaving together pieces of different faiths. She argued that in creating a spiritual tapestry from different religious persuasions people may be tempted to absorb ideas that are expedient or intellectually tantalizing, while rejecting practices that require effort or discipline. Her own fascination with Christianity was initially aroused through her romantic involvement with a Christian man, but was sustained after the relationship ended. Although this woman desired to expand the boundaries of her Jewish heritage, she did not wish to renounce her primary religious identity. She was seeking to assimilate Christian ideals that would complement, but not compromise, her allegiance to the Jewish faith.

This student's concerns are worthy of further reflection. Attempting to merge highly divergent religious philosophies is not an easy task. Moreover, spiritual eclecticism is not necessarily indicative of greater maturity. While openness to disparate religious world views can be a sign of mature faith, it can also be used to avoid discipline and commitment or to justify unwholesome life styles. This kind of extrinsic spiritual eclecticism is psychospiritually immature. However, we can enhance our faith by selectively assimilating ideals that progress our spiritual development and relationship to God.

5. *A mature faith is purged of egocentricity, magical thinking and anthropomorphisms.* Much has been said about this criterion in previous chapters. In less mature stages of spiritual development, religious involvement is used to console a broken spirit or to quell neurotic fears. God images of those with a less evolved religious capacity are either severely fragmented or merged with early object representations.

The spiritually mature, on the other hand, transcend the self through their commitment to a higher power. Their God images are unfettered by childhood identifications and projections to the extent that this disentanglement is humanly possible. However constrained by the limits of human vision, these extraordinary individuals are privileged to catch a glimpse of the kingdom of God.

6. *Reason and emotion are both essential to a mature spiritual outlook.* Contemplation of human existence leads to troublesome and philosophically complex dilemmas such as the inevitability of death, the purpose of tragedy and suffering and the problem of good and evil. Religious groups that foster a romanticized vision of the human predicament make a mockery of real hardship and blame victims for their suffering. Travelers on the road to mature faith have the courage to ask the profound existential questions without expecting easy answers.

The spiritually immature seek comfort and security through blind faith or unquestioning loyalty to a religious authority. However, faith that reduces existential dilemmas to simple formulas provides little more than a temporary spiritual intoxicant for the religiously naive. Despite the fact that fundamentalist groups resent accusations that religion functions as a crutch for the emotionally immature, they promote less mature forms of religiousness by discouraging the creative questioning and intellectual exploration that lead to internalization and integration of spiritual values. The suspension of critical thinking and logical reasoning that is common in these religious communities contributes to fanaticism and narrow-mindedness.

Mystical approaches to spirituality also deemphasize the intellectual dimension not to avoid complex issues, but because the sacred is approached through nonrational experiences and extreme emotional states. For the mystic a meeting of the Divine is attained through heightened affect and altered states of consciousness, rather than through intellectual contemplation. However, when the authenticity of spiritual insight is judged by the intensity of feeling, one's religious life may become a search for emotional excitement. Attempts to feel more spiritual through mind-altering drugs, masochistic ascetic practices or morbid introspection are more a self-centered preoccupation with emotional highs than a genuine spiritual quest.

On the other hand, human reason alone is insufficient to engage one's spiritual sensibilities. A feeling of devotion to God is as essential to a healthy spiritual life as a rational philosophical underpinning. Religious communities that arouse sentiments of reverence and human compassion are more likely to inspire commitment and wholesome living than those that appeal exclusively to the intellect. James's dictum that "emotion convicts before logic convinces" suggests that in order to take root, faith must first capture the heart.

7. *A healthy spiritual life is characterized by mature concern for others.* Fromm proposed that the most important characteristic of mature faith is a sustained sense of responsibility and deep compassion for others.[11] He firmly believed that a mature religious quest is not a search for personal enlightenment, but a striving to contribute to the betterment of humankind. The goal of the spiritual life is stated in Jesus' command to "love thy neighbor as thyself."

If authoritarian religions are guilty of promoting a self-effacing attitude that undermines the individual's self-esteem, some humanistic traditions exalt the individual to narcissistic extremes. Similarly, the faith of the mystic, if predominantly focused on intense, altered states of consciousness, may encourage a self-centered search for spiritual highs. Theologian Kenneth Leech reminds us that "the great masters of the spiritual life in almost all traditions are one in warning of the dangers of the spiritual ego-trip, the search for enlightenment which ignores . . . the human community."[12]

The spiritually mature "bear the fruits" of faithful living through community involvement and selfless devotion to universal ideals. Such persons speak boldly against injustice and work tirelessly toward their visions of a transformed world. Their ultimate respect for people of all faiths derives from their extraordinary capacity to empathize with the commonwealth of being.

8. *Mature faith supports tolerance, human growth and celebration of life.* Those at the apex of spiritual development are not perfect people and are keenly aware of their personal vulnerabilities and limitations. They are humble enough to accept responsibility for wrongdoing and to make restitution whenever possible. At the same time, people with spiritual vision do not insist on perfection and can forgive themselves and others for their failures and liabilities. Mature faith is both self-accepting and self-progressing.

Religions that accentuate the depravity and sinfulness of humankind mistakenly assume that spiritual humbleness is fashioned from humiliation and shame. These groups are convinced that the individual will turn to God only after he or she is stripped of dignity and self-worth. By weakening the human spirit and sacralizing self-contempt, a sin-focused religiosity has devastating effects on the person's psychological and spiritual development.

A mature spiritual quest does not constrict the personality into watertight compartments. Progression beyond superego religion directs individuals toward organizing all aspects of personhood into an integrated and unified whole. This celebration of selfhood does not mean that every impulse and desire should be indiscriminately indulged. People with spiritual passion have a strong moral fiber that helps them to express normal human needs and desires in ways that are life-enhancing and congruent with their values. At stage five spontaneity and pleasure-seeking coexist with self-discipline and appropriate restraint. Neither overindulgence nor extreme self-denial is a feature of mature faith.

9. *A mature spiritual outlook acknowledges the reality of evil and suffering.* James distinguished "healthy minded" religion from the religious outlook of the "sick soul."[13] These labels are deceptive in that the outlook of the sick soul is, in some respects, emotionally healthier than the naive optimism of the healthy minded. In its extreme form, as in Christian Science and positive-thinking cults, healthy minded faith is a system of denial. By acting as if evil does not exist and all problems are surmountable through mentalism, these groups promote a religion of human omnipotence. Loathe to acknowledge that there are circumstances over which individuals have little or no control, disciples of mind-cure or positive thinking inadvertently blame the virtuous for their suffering.

Another way of persuading ourselves that evil does not exist is to believe that all suffering happens for good reasons. Proponents of this "healthy minded" philosophy seek to convince the sick and the aggrieved that their anguish is a contribution toward some ultimate good. This argument has a kernel of truth in that some people have survived unconscionable abuses by finding a purpose for their suffering. Nevertheless, it makes a mockery of our sense of justice and fairness to assume that all personal misfortune is in the service of some universal goodness. Violent acts and senseless tragedies are never blessings in disguise.

Evil and violence are social realities that cannot be magically erased through positive thinking. Yet sometimes an attitude of humble acceptance is the best weapon against feelings of helplessness and despair. The miracle of faith is that by acknowledging the limitations of our ability to endure extraordinary heartbreak, we find unexpected courage and perseverance from a source outside of ourselves.[14]

The religious melancholy of the "sick soul" stands in radical opposition to the exaggerated optimism of the healthy minded. Attuned to the precariousness of human destiny, the morbid minded are tormented by existential anxiety and sadness. Although extreme sensitivity to life's cruelty and hardship can lead to unmitigated cynicism and a cheerless existence, the consciousness of evil that characterizes the sick soul, if balanced by a capacity to experience pleasure, is psychologically healthier than the Pollyanna vision of the healthy minded.

A life-affirming spiritual philosophy inspires an optimistic outlook without denying the reality of evil, tragedy and suffering. While recognizing that death and misfortune are an inevitable part of the human experience, the spiritually mature also feel empowered by an essential goodness and infinite power that they call God.

10. *Mature faith provides an overarching meaning and purpose.* Each of us seeks to discover a purpose in life and a meaning for our existence. For those attuned to a higher consciousness, faith provides an overarching meaning that directs their energy, relates them to God and propels them toward universal ideals.

It is this compelling sense of being summoned to participate in a larger purpose that gives faith its vitality and power to transform human lives. By inspiring efforts to fulfill a higher meaning, faith binds us as a human community and makes us all co-workers in performing God's work on earth.

11. *Mature faith leaves ample room for both traditional beliefs and private interpretations.* Faith can be nourished and vitalized through religious observance. However, when doctrine is central to the spiritual enterprise, it provides the foundation, but not the essence, of one's faith. The spiritually mature who are committed to a religious tradition subscribe to their beliefs with a tentativeness and an openness that permit them to incorporate new ideas that may complement, expand or revise their spiritual understanding.

James, distinguishing between religion as an "individual personal function" and religion as an "institutional product" and believing formal religion to be inferior to personal revelation, confined his treatise to first-hand religious experiences. He believed that "ecclesiastical or theological complications" contaminate the nucleus of the spiritual life, which is "the consciousness which individuals have of an intercourse between themselves and higher powers with which they feel themselves to be related."[15] Others have supported the notion that "individual religion is much superior to institutional religion, for religion must start with faith, and faith must start from within."[16]

Religionists and religious sympathizers who oppose this viewpoint argue that faith is rooted in divine revelation. A spiritual world view that is formulated from personal experience or ideas from divergent sources is abominable to those who believe that the religious scriptures and doctrines of a particular tradition proclaim the will of the sovereign God. Yet even the most fundamentalistic religious groups succumb to what James calls "secular alterations."

For example, since the rise of the feminist movement women are no longer restricted to subordinate roles in their religious communities. Sanctions against divorce, remarriage and homosexuality have also been lifted in many traditions. I can remember when churches ostracized divorced members. Today, most religious groups not only accept the divorced and remarried into their fold, but also perform wedding ceremonies for congregation members entering into second marriages. Similarly, most religious traditions are no longer unanimous in their condemnation of homosexuality as evidenced by the emergence of denominational affiliated groups for gays and lesbians such as Dignity (Catholic) and Evangelicals Concerned.

These examples indicate that religious codes are shaped, at least in part, by prevailing cultural norms. As changes occur in the social structure of the Western world, religious doctrines are modified to fit the thinking and mood of the times. Since absolute truth is presumably unalterable, such modifications and reformulations suggest that no religious group at any particular time can claim to be the sole interpreter of God's purpose. Progressive congregations in all religious traditions allow some flexibility of interpretation.

Religious groups and denominations that pretend to possess infallible knowledge thwart the spiritual development of our generation. The idealism and discovery of the sacred that flow from creative thinking and critical exploration are sacrificed for the illusion of certitude. Formal worship and ritual become substitutes for meaningful experience. When individuals are absorbed into the corporate mind of the religious institution, their interior lives become shallow and lifeless.

In admitting that some religious groups promote elitism and intolerance, we must be cautious not to become cynical toward all traditional religion. Every religious tradition is represented by both oppressive and progressive sectors. Despite the flaws of our religious institutions there are distinct advantages to having a religious identity and belonging to a religious community. In addition, those of us who are biased toward private spirituality may overlook the disadvantages of rugged individualism.

It is true that faith that is fashioned from convictions of the heart and ideas from diverse traditions is fresh, vital and relevant. At its best, private religion transforms the human spirit and inspires true saintliness. It flourishes in those who see that a variety of spiritual paths contain a universal message. In those with less developed spiritual sensitivities, private religion can be motivated by fear of commitment or compulsive self-reliance. In their determination to escape the tyranny of dogma, compulsive individualists sacrifice the sense of spiritual solidarity that develops among a community of believers. Because of their reluctance to commit to anything, they also fail to establish a unifying philosophy of life that provides spiritual and moral direction.

Spiritual growth is nurtured in human relationships through interpersonal sharing and trust. A faith community invites its members to join together in expressing and symbolizing their devotion and loyalty to God and the commonwealth of being. Our most significant spiritual experiences have their greatest impact when shared with others. Indeed, our major religions derived from the private revelations of spiritually gifted individuals.   Had Jesus, Saint Paul, Buddha, Mohammad, Abraham or Moses merely reveled in his own spiritual enlightenment, humankind would have been deprived of its profound religious heritage. Moreover, when personal insights are subjected to the critical eye of others, they are less likely to be molded to fit self-centered interests.

Gordon Allport believed that the maturity of our faith is judged on the basis not of *what* we believe, but of *how* we believe, and that intrinsically committed people can be counted among the traditionally religious as well as those who choose a more solitary path.[17] Mature faith leaves ample room for both traditional beliefs and private experience. Those of us who are inspired by a particular theology must cultivate a sensitivity to our inner spiritual voices in order to resist the temptation to externalize and dogmatize our faith. Conversely, it behooves those of us who choose a solitary path to expand our spiritual boundaries through open dialogue with members of traditional religious faiths.

NOTES

1. William James, *The Varieties of Religious Experience* (New York: Penguin Books, 1985), 274.

2. Erich Fromm, *Psychoanalysis and Religion* (New Haven, Conn.: Yale University Press, 1950).

3. Ibid., 37, 93.

4. James, *Varieties,* 513.

5. Ibid., 508.

6. Carl Jung, *Psychology and Religion* (New Haven, Conn.: Yale University Press, 1938).

7. John Hoyland, trans., "Song by Tukaram," in *An Indian Peasant Mystic* (London: Allenson, 1932).

8. Gordon Allport, *The Individual and His Religion* (New York: Macmillan, 1950), 83.

9. Mahatma Gandhi, *Gandhi's Autobiography: The Story of My Experiments with Truth* (Washington, D.C.: Public Affairs Press, 1948), 5.

10. Fromm, *Psychoanalysis and Religion*, 113.

11. Ibid.

12. Kenneth Leech, *Soul Friend: The Practice of Christian Spirituality* (London: Sheldon Press, 1977), 38.

13. James, *Varieties.*

14. The reader is referred to Viktor Frankl, *Man's Search for Meaning* (New York: Simon & Schuster, 1963); and Harold Kushner, *When Bad Things Happen to Good People* (New York: Avon Books, 1981), for a more in-depth discussion of these issues.

15. James, *Varieties*, 465.

16. George Anderson, *Your Religion: Neurotic or Healthy?* (Garden City, N.Y.: Doubleday, 1970), 181.

17. Gordon Allport, "Behavioral Science, Religion, and Mental Health," *Journal of Religion and Health* 2 (1963): 187-197.

Epilogue

The operating assumption of this book is that the faith of spiritually committed individuals is profoundly influenced by their personal histories. Whether the sacred is felt to be wholly other or to reside within the self, the individual's experience of the human-Divine encounter is molded by his or her psychological economy. Therefore, therapists and counselors who wish to cure the defects of the spiritual life must help troubled seekers heal their emotional wounds and fractures. I have provided a stage model of faith to assist professional caregivers with this difficult task.

It is not my intent to preempt other developmental typologies of faith or religious experience. Each provides a unique perspective on how individuals confront the ultimate conditions of existence throughout the life span. My goal has been to call attention to how our formative relationships contribute to the ways in which we respond to the creative life force that we call God.

A psychology of faith provides a glimmer of insight into that which is essentially inscrutable. However influenced by developmental events and therapeutic interventions, it would be preposterous to presume that the individual's relationship to the sacred is entirely psychologically determined. That the highest forms of nobility and saintliness have flourished in people who suffered unfathomable abuses and hardship forces us to acknowledge the limitations of our theories and constructs. The working of God's grace in the human spirit eludes psychological analysis. It is the miracle of faith.

Bibliography

Allport, Gordon. *The Individual and His Religion*. New York: Macmillan, 1950.

———. "Behavioral Science, Religion, and Mental Health." *Journal of Religion and Health* 2 (1963): 187-197.

Allport, Gordon, and J. Michael Ross. "Personal Religious Orientation and Prejudice." *Journal of Personality and Social Psychology* 5 (1967): 432-443.

Anderson, George. *Your Religion: Neurotic or Healthy?* Garden City, N.Y.: Doubleday, 1970.

Batson, C. Daniel, and W. Larry Ventis. *The Religious Experience: A Social-Psychological Perspective*. New York: Oxford University Press, 1982.

Benson, Herbert. *Beyond the Relaxation Response*. New York: Berkley Books, 1985.

Blanck, Gertrude, and Rubin Blanck. *Ego Psychology: Theory and Practice*. New York: Columbia University Press, 1974.

Bradford, David. "A Therapy of Religious Imagery for Paranoid Schizophrenic Psychosis." In *Psychotherapy of the Religious Patient*, ed. M. Spero, 154-180. Springfield, Il.: Charles C. Thomas, 1985.

Clark, Walter Houston. *The Psychology of Religion*. New York: Macmillan, 1958.

Corey, Gerald. *The Theory and Practice of Group Counseling*. Monterey, Calif.: Brooks/Cole, 1985.

Donahue, Michael. "Intrinsic and Extrinsic Religiousness: Review and Meta-Analysis." *Journal of Personality and Social Psychology* 48 (1985): 400-419.

Ellis, Albert. "Psychotherapy and Atheistic Values: A Response to A.E. Bergin's 'Psychotherapy and Religious Values.' " *Journal of Consulting and Clinical Psychology* 48 (1980): 635-639.

Emmons, Michael, and Rev. David Richardson. *The Assertive Christian.* Minneapolis, Minn.: Winston Press, 1981.

Finn, Mark, and John Gartner, eds. *Object Relations Theory and Religion.* Westport, Conn.: Praeger, 1992.

Fowler, James. *Stages of Faith: The Psychology of Human Development and the Quest for Meaning.* San Francisco: Harper & Row, 1981.

Frankl, Viktor. *Man's Search for Meaning.* New York: Simon & Schuster, 1963.

Freud, Sigmund. *The Future of an Illusion.* New York: Doubleday, 1927.

Fromm, Erich. *Psychoanalysis and Religion.* New Haven, Conn.: Yale University Press, 1950.

Gandhi, Mahatma. *Gandhi's Autobiography: The Story of My Experiments with Truth.* Washington, D.C.: Public Affairs Press, 1948.

Genia, Vicky. "Religious Development: Synthesis and Reformulation." *Journal of Religion and Health* 29 (1990): 85-99.

———. "Interreligious Encounter Group: A Psychospiritual Experience for Faith Development." *Counseling and Values* 35 (1990): 39-51.

———. "Psychospiritual Group Counseling for College Students." *Journal for College Student Development* 31 (1990): 279-280.

———. "Religious Imagery of a Schizotypal Patient." *Journal of Religion and Health* 31 (1992): 317-326.

———. "Transitional Faith: A Developmental Step Toward Religious Maturity." *Counseling and Values* 37 (1992): 15-24.

Gilligan, Carol. *In a Different Voice.* Cambridge: Harvard University Press, 1982.

Goodman-Malamuth, Leslie, and Robin Margolis. *Between Two Worlds: Choices for Grown Children of Jewish-Christian Parents.* New York: Pocket Books, 1992.

Hadaway, C. Kirk. "Identifying American Apostates: A Cluster Analysis." *Journal for the Scientific Study of Religion* 28 (1989): 201-215.

Hoyland, John, trans. "Song by Tukaram." In *An Indian Peasant Mystic.* London: Allenson, 1932.

James, William. *The Varieties of Religious Experience.* New York: Penguin Books, 1985.

Jones, James. *Contemporary Psychoanalysis and Religion.* New Haven, Conn.: Yale University Press, 1991.

———. "Living on the Boundary Between Psychology and Religion." *Psychology of Religion Newsletter, American Psychological Association Division 36* 18 (1993): 1-7.

Jung, Carl. *Psychology and Religion*. New Haven, Conn.: Yale University Press, 1938.

Kernberg, Otto. *Borderline Conditions and Pathological Narcissism*. New York: Jason Aronson, 1985.

Klieger, James. "Emerging from the 'Dark Night of the Soul': Healing the False Self in a Narcissistically Vulnerable Minister." *Psychoanalytic Psychology* 7 (1990): 211-224.

Kohlberg, Lawrence. *The Psychology of Moral Development*. San Francisco: Harper & Row, 1984.

Kunkel, Fritz. *Let's Be Normal*. New York: Ives Washburn, 1929.

Kushner, Harold. *When Bad Things Happen to Good People*. New York: Avon Books, 1981.

Lande, Nathaniel, and Afton Slade. *Stages: Understanding How You Make Your Moral Decisions*. San Francisco: Harper & Row, 1979.

Leech, Kenneth. *Soul Friend: The Practice of Christian Spirituality*. London: Sheldon Press, 1977.

Lovinger, Robert. *Working with Religious Issues in Therapy*. New York: Jason Aronson, 1984.

———. "Religious Imagery in the Psychotherapy of a Borderline Patient." In *Psychotherapy of the Religious Patient*, ed. M. Spero, 181-207. Springfield, Il.: Charles C. Thomas, 1985.

Mahler, Margaret, Fred Pine and Anni Bergman. *The Psychological Birth of the Human Infant*. New York: Basic Books, 1975.

Rizutto, Ana-Maria. *The Birth of the Living God*. Chicago: University of Chicago Press, 1979.

Schumaker, John, ed. *Religion and Mental Health*. New York: Oxford University Press, 1992.

Spero, Moshe, ed. *Psychotherapy of the Religious Patient*. Springfield, Il.: Charles C. Thomas, 1985.

Starbuck, Edwin. *The Psychology of Religion*. New York: Scribner, 1899.

Tan, Siang-Yang. "Explicit Integration in Psychotherapy." Paper presented at the International Congress on Christian Counseling, Counseling and Spirituality Track, Atlanta, November 1988.

Tillich, Paul. *The Dynamics of Faith*. New York: Harper & Row, 1957.

Watson, P.J., Robin Howard, Ralph Hood and Ronald Morris. "Age and Religious Orientation." *Review of Religious Research* 29 (1988): 271-280.

Wulff, David. *Psychology of Religion: Classic and Contemporary Views*. New York: Wiley, 1991.

Yalom, Irvin. *The Theory and Practice of Group Psychotherapy*. New York: Basic Books, 1975.

Index

About the Author

VICKY GENIA is a psychologist at the American University Center for Psychological and Learning Services in Washington, D.C. She has written well-received articles on psychospiritual counseling, one of which will be published in *Counseling: The Spiritual Dimension* (1995).

ISBN 0-275-95107-3

HARDCOVER BAR CODE